DIVORCE — VATICAN STYLE

DIVORCE—
VATICAN STYLE

Oliver Stewart

OLIPHANTS

OLIPHANTS
BLUNDELL HOUSE
GOODWOOD ROAD
LONDON S.E.14

ISBN 0 551 00069 4
Printed in Great Britain by
Butler & Tanner Ltd, Frome and London

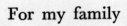

For my family

Contents

Contents

Introduction

Italy, a country which has bound itself to accept the rules of the Roman Catholic Church, is falling away from strict adherence. New civil laws affecting divorce—unthinkable in Vatican eyes—are providing a possible solution to unwanted marriage. The tyranny of enforced union is ending.

Discussing this, the British *Catholic Herald* newspaper last year commented: 'divorce—Italian style—is a nonsense'. It may be, but is divorce, Vatican style, any better?

At a time when the Pope is leading his Church towards closer ecumenical union with the rest of the Christian world, the basic difference of viewpoint on this tortured subject threatens to enlarge rather than reduce the gulf between them.

Inside the Roman Church, too, great dissension exists. Canon law, in the better-developed industrial nations of the West, is being increasingly criticised and disregarded on this point.

Thus the aim of this book is to examine and explain the effect of the law on some who have come into conflict with it.

9

'. . . the sacrament of Marriage, being instituted for the preservation and increase of the human race, has a necessary relation to the circumstances of life which, though connected with marriage, belong to the civil order, and about which the State rightly makes inquiry . . .'

POPE LEO XIII

ONE

The Bond

Late in 1963 when Lee Radziwill, sister of Jackie Kennedy, was given a decree of nullity proving that her first marriage had never happened, some forty thousand marriage cases were settling like autumn leaves in the nooks and crannies of the marriage courts of the Roman Catholic World. Of these, six hundred or so were piled on the crowded tables of the Sacred Roman Rota in Rome, the Church's highest appeal court. A whole host more were in stages of preparation at village priest level from Bokhara to Buenos Aires.

For anyone with the gift of imagination, it is slightly horrifying to consider the sum of human unhappiness locked up in these mysterious and often futile petitions. To try to assess the depths of frustration and envy—let alone astonishment—brought to their authors by publication of the favourable Radziwill verdict is to attempt the impossible.

The predictable consequence of the suit was a swelling chorus of anxious voices, both inside the Church and out, pressing for an alteration in the marriage laws and the way they are administered. How long before such alterations are considered, let alone adopted, is another matter, but in Italy today we are seeing a beginning. There the revolutionary tide may seem to be on the turn, if not already coming in fast. Meanwhile, the tragedies continue.

In the Catholic Church such agonies of **mind and**

conscience as are constantly evoked by the marriage laws command no special sympathy from the celibate priests who administer the verdicts of the courts. The nature of marriage being understood, there is no reason why they should. Nevertheless, the Church *is* concerned about the growing tug-of-war between what Catholics ought to do in marriage and what they do do. Far too many RCs are known to be weighing the laws of the Church against the call of their senses and going along, loosely, with St Paul's preference for matrimony rather than conflagration. But without the blessing of their Church.

Where they are married, and it is not possible to untie both legal and ecclesiastical knots, they tend increasingly to settle for the former. In America, a canon law professor, the Rev. William Bassett, has quantified the problem. 'Perhaps as many as a million adults every year in the United States cease to share the Holy Eucharist in Communion with the Catholic Church, because they cannot sustain a permanent marriage,' he was reported as having said recently.

'To those who suffer in isolated loneliness,' he continued, 'to those who are abandoned or who live in snakepits of hostility, it is not enough any more to appeal to the authority of the Church's law. This law and its authority can no longer help to preserve the holiness of marriage for the vast majority of mankind.'

Another American, confessor to the late Pope John and internationally well-known moral theologian Father Bernard Haring, reportedly wrote in a memorandum last year to the Canon Law Society of America: 'I want to stress the point that in matters of conscience we cannot overlook the fact that a very great sector of Catholics are not, and cannot be, convinced that a totally-destroyed previous marriage should hinder them forever from entering a new marital relationship.'

12

There are more than five hundred million Roman Catholics in the world. They constitute a sixth of the population. They are not only the most plentiful but also the largest power group ever to have existed on this planet. As Catholics, they must believe in the absolute rule that marriage is for ever. Their Church holds it to be God's will that no baptised, married Christian can ever destroy the sacrament of marriage. Not only may they not marry again, *but they may never divorce*.

Though legal separations are approved and sanctioned by the Church, these do not end the bond of marriage. A separated man and wife live as strangers together or, as the Church defines the relationship, 'like brother and sister', yet are still married. In all practical ways, they may have parted. Perhaps their lives have become totally separate. Financially they may be self-supporting, and children of the marrige may either be shared, or brought up by one of the partners. Yet they are man and wife as surely and irrevocably as when they knelt at God's altar to receive the sacramental blessing on their union. One flesh: absolute, eternal —and, in the Catholic Church, unrepeatable.

Ah, you ask, but surely there are Holy Romans who have obtained a divorce, or something of the sort, from the Vatican? What of these? Is there not something known as 'nullity'? Have we not heard of these 'nullities' being handed out in Rome to any number of rich and celebrated Catholic couples? What about that fantastic Marconi case in history? And how did the American heiress, Consuela Vanderbilt, *divorce* the Duke of Marlborough some years ago if not by this special dispensation given to Catholics who want to break their marriage chains?

We will consider these cases. But first, let us understand the true basis of Roman Catholic marriage. When a Roman Catholic marries within the Church, that is to say with the Church's sanction, then he or she has applied directly to

God (in the presence of an officer of the Church, as witness) for what Catholics know to be 'the sacrament of matrimony'. If no obstacle to the marriage exists—what the Church would call an impediment—and if the marriage is subsequently consummated by an act of physical love, then the sacrament is granted and the bond sealed. It becomes a spiritual union: holy, eternal and irrevocable.

To understand this fully we must get to grips with this mystical 'sacrament', which Catholics believe to be the basis of all Christian marriage. In total, there are seven sacraments in the Church. There is probably no way of stating simply what they are, except that they are supreme gifts of God.

The sacraments are baptism, confirmation, confession, the Holy Eucharist or Communion, Holy Orders, matrimony and the anointing of the sick. Via any of these, Catholic men and women may enter into a pact with God, in which they receive highly favoured consideration. But, equally essentially, the sacraments are understandable only in terms of another mystical condition, the 'state of grace'. This is where a Catholic is purified so that 'God can enter in'. In such a state all blemishes are believed to disappear. All is scoured and cleansed by confession, absolution and communion.

Thus, in the case of marriage, the sacrament becomes available only to those who are fully eligible and ready for it. These are the couples who are making their marriage vows in absolute honesty and sincerity of purpose, with purity of mind and body. Yet both the husband and wife in such a marriage must understand the meaning and responsibility entailed by their vows.

For, once the sacrament has been granted to them, they will enter a further 'state of grace', and this will support them for as long as they live according to their vows, and the vows of the Church. It will make their union unshatterable and everlasting. To betray it is to commit a deadly sin.

Thus, the Catholic marriage courts have no power to break these marriage bonds, even when good cause may seem to exist for doing so. Indeed they *cannot* break them, since no man can put a married couple asunder. The courts are simply there to decide whether or not the sacrament has been granted, in cases where there is subsequent and reasonable doubt.

These are the courts which often seem so heartless, but they have no power to be otherwise. Their function, when anyone applies to them for permission to be free of an unwanted marriage, is to adjudicate only on God's behalf. As far as it is possible for men to do so, their judges must debate whether or not the spiritual sacrament was granted to a couple. If they decide that it was, then the marriage must stand. If not, then it is null.

In such cases, the couple not only *are* not married. They never have been married. If they have children, these have been born out of wedlock. In effect, they do not legally exist. This means that where a man or woman enters marriage without being in the 'state of grace' (i.e. pure in intention, mind and body) then there is no marriage. It is without the spiritual bond of God's sacrament. It never happened.

For Protestants to question this is natural, but not as original as might be supposed. Theologians, popes and scholars of the Roman Church have been defining and re-defining the sacraments with unending vigour since medieval times. In marriage there has always been a smoulder of doubt among the theologians. It is because the sacrament has to be bestowed, so to speak, in two parts.

Try to understand the Church's dilemma over this. Marriage, in Catholic eyes, is essentially a procreative union. The act of sexual intercourse is therefore vital to the bond, hence to the sacrament. But should two people who have married properly, yet who have never consummated their union, remain married? Are they fully bound to one another in God's eyes. This is the nub of the problem which has disturbed Catholic thinkers for generations. The final ruling is that marriage is not entered into where there has been no honest intention to 'make matters right'.

The phrase is well-chosen. It means that non-consummation *by itself* does not constitute an automatic ground for nullifying the marriage. Not unless there is, and always has been, refusal on the part of one or other of the partners to make physical love, and when this refusal will persist indefinitely. The interesting point here is that such marriages do take place. They are half-tied knots only, but they exist. Perhaps it can be said that the sacrament was received in them, but not fully committed.

To deal with this curious position, the Pope has special 'vicarious powers'. They allow him to dispense what non-Catholics mistakenly might think of as 'divorce'. He *can* dissolve a true marriage by putting it aside. And he may leave the parties free to marry again.

Two other conditions exist in which Catholics, in extremely rare instances, may be granted a similar form of 'divorce'. Known as the Pauline and the Petrine privileges, after Saints Paul and Peter, these are complex mysteries of Catholic legal theology which a leading Catholic editor says 'nobody really understands'. They refer strictly and solely to cases where both or one party to the assumed marriage was unbaptised. It cannot be said too clearly, or too often, that *in no other case* can a Catholic married couple on whom the sacrament has been bestowed ever hope to end their marriage.

What we shall investigate here is the involved and sometimes extraordinary conduct of those who seek, through the Catholic marriage courts, to prove that their marriages never were sacramental bonds at all.

TWO

What is Marriage?

There are major criticisms of the Roman Catholic marriage courts from both sides of the fence, from inside as well as outside the Vatican stockade. They castigate delays which are especially hurtful to young Catholics whose passions are involved, but whose whole freedom and hope of eventual spiritual happiness lies in the Church. They also condemn the many instances of apparent favour for those in high places.

The following was written forty years ago by the celebrated free-thinker, Bertrand Russell: 'The Catholic Church, on the ground that marriage is a sacrament, does not allow divorce for any purpose whatsoever, but in practice this severity is somewhat mitigated—especially where the great ones of the earth are concerned . . .'

Today, such criticism can be traced to many Catholic sources as well. Yet a much more cogent complaint attacks the wrappings of secrecy which swathe and swaddle these courts, shutting out every glimmer of information about their inner workings.

Such secrecy envelops the Rota in Rome that even its personal staff of loyal clerks, all priests versed in canon law and under oath not to reveal the court's affairs, are forbidden to know the texts of certain verdicts. Of the rancour aroused by these repressive methods, the Church pretends to be aware. In reality it is no better informed, or guided, than any other vast, administrative complex.

17

The sighs of self-reproach, so easy to overhear in the corridors of the Roman curia, are honest expressions of men who realise the imperfections of their machinery. Yet a widespread conviction among officials that the Church is helplessly innocent in matters of public and press relations is considerably overstated. In fact, the Church shows itself better able to exploit popular and colourful occasions, such as the Pope's occasional visits to popular tourist resorts, than any power in the world with the possible exception of Soviet Russia.

It has to be understood that the secrecy which upsets and offends many faithful Catholics is a deliberate factor in the Church's central policy. Indeed, secrecy is part of the central idea of a sophisticated faith in which such mystical gifts-from-God as sacraments are to be found. Because the sacrament is not an easily explicable thing, even for a true believer, it needs special consideration based on unshake-able, logical reasoning, and part of this is the clear and sensible belief that overmuch revelation can be harmful, both for the individuals concerned and for the Church. Secrecy is therefore an end in itself.

Where participants in a nullity suit are celebrated figures, argues the Church, any disclosure of intimate details in their lives is bound to attract prurient and vulgar curiosity. This can do nothing but harm. To protect such celebrities and, at the same time, to shield themselves from ignorant abuse and misunderstanding, the marriage courts wrap themselves in elaborate silence.

It is this which has provoked irritation and frustration, more so than any other aspect of Catholic marriage. There are many who believe it is needlessly distorting and unfairly discriminating. It is certainly thought to be out-moded. But the Church and its officers hold the view that almost total secrecy is an essential climate for the most delicate and private cases.

Without the security of darkness, they stress, the workings of the courts, in upholding God's laws, would be as seriously hampered as if, say, a surgeon had to perform an operation without anaesthetic. Thus, before attempting analysis of the processes by which the Sacred Rota and the marriage courts function, we must try to understand the inner nature of this marriage union. It can so easily and lightly be entered into; yet it so often produces the most dire and complicated results. What are its properties, and how do they differ in the eyes of different Christian sects?

We know that over all Christian marriage stands the injunction of Christ: 'Those whom God hath joined together, let no man put asunder.' We are aware that the Catholic Church has interpreted this literally, as meaning that no divorce is or ever can be tolerated of a marriage which has God's full approval.

At the same time we realise that dissenting Christians allow a more generous interpretation of the edict, and that for many it is doubtful even if Jesus Christ intended to place a lasting stricture on the marriage union. But, in one thing, all Christians agree—marriage follows nature. It is the highest form of natural law, involving free selection and a union from which future life must emerge unimpeded.

A leading Catholic writer has defined Christian marriage as the perfection of that form of union which is natural to man. This would not be disputed by non-Catholics. If the Church of Rome were to see itself only as the true, appointed guardian of this natural law, as well as of 'God's positive ordinances', that would be acceptable to all. But it does, of course, go very much further than that.

One is almost led to the belief that Catholic theologians interpret sexual intercourse as sin, whether or not it is for the purpose of procreation. Their scale of virtuous priorities certainly places abstinence, such as the celibacy of priests and nuns of the Church, above happy and fulfilled marriage. Sexual love is always 'original sin', despite its necessary and greatly urged end in reproduction. Outside the Roman Church this is hard to understand, but it must be noted in any consideration of the treatment which the bonds of marriage receive in the Catholic courts.

The viewpoint here seems to be that sexual pleasure is a necessary evil, undergone only for the blessed purpose of producing children, and of harmonising the marriage union through this pursuit. Any suggestion that marriage may also countenance a sexual playground between man and woman appears to be opposed to the whole concept, although the Vatican Council has ruled that one may enjoy sex for itself.

Catholics, therefore, should not too openly enjoy their love-making. Nor must they hinder, in any but a purely natural way, the procreation of children as a result of their intercourse. Indeed, by discovering a drug, taken orally, which is capable of delaying the period of female ovulation, science has produced a shattering poser for Catholic theologians.

How they will finally equate it with their basic principles is a matter of considerable interest to an over-crowded world. If the urge to copulate is to be licensed by marriage, as well as the need to do so in order to produce children, then the whole conception of Catholic sin will be seriously disturbed. It is one thing for Catholics who feel themselves prevented from child-bearing, by reasons of poverty, health or mere inclination, to practise the 'rhythm method' (cynically termed 'Vatican Roulette'). It is quite another matter for Catholic husbands and wives to be given what might well become total sexual freedom with no other purpose in mind.

Denial of the latter while approving the former has already brought a torrent of criticism of the Church. It could well open the way for a revolutionary re-appraisal of

Catholic marriage, which radicals believe to be overdue. Aside from its sexual element, Christian marriage differs mainly in terms of the authority which is given power over it. For Catholics, the Church has always asserted its right to total control over the application or removal of the sacramental bond. It has done so by virtue of its position as God's appointed Church.

Dissenters, on the other hand, allow the State to control the law of marriage as a contract. They reserve for themselves only the performance and celebration of its rites. Hence the laws of countries which do not accept the authority of Rome frequently differ from those of their Catholic compatriots. And these distinctions do nothing to ease the Roman Catholic Church's control over more wayward members of its flock.

As a result of this, many Catholics obtain civil divorces in the lands where they live, while remaining married in the eyes and laws of the Church of Rome. At the same time married non-Catholics, if baptised in their Churches, are recognised by Rome as having been 'joined in a sacramental union'.

Should they divorce civilly, their broken marriage is *not* recognised by Rome. Thus neither party is eligible for remarriage to a Catholic with Church approval. By these and other differences, Church and State have been drawn into conflicts which have pursued them through the centuries, and which have recently brought turmoil to Italy. It may be remembered that in England, Cardinal Wolsey's advocacy and King Henry VIII's desire for a son similarly combined to overthrow the rule of the Church of Rome.

Today in America, the United States are singularly divided in their attitude to marriage and divorce. So that North Carolina agrees with Rome in refusing to legalise divorce, while in the State of Nevada a civil dissolution may be obtained for a wide and tolerant variety of causes, including 'gross drunkenness'.

Although the widely-dispersed Catholic flock is exposed to this variety of viewpoints, their Church demands their absolute obedience to the laws of God as interpreted in Rome. 'Marriage', wrote F. J. Sheed, the Catholic lawyer, scholar and publisher, 'is a relationship (God-made) resulting from a contract (man-made) . . . the law of divorce concerns the *relationship*: the law of nullity concerns the *contract*. The difference between divorce and nullity is therefore about as wide as it is possible to conceive. Divorce claims to break up a marriage actually in being. Nullity means that the marriage never came into being; it is the discovery that the contract to marry did not exist. Marriage is not *only* a contract; but it results from a contract, and if there is no contract, no relationship can result.'*

Though it is rarely in dispute among Christians, there is a further fact to be taken into consideration: the acceptance of monogamy. The Catholic Church is firmly of the opinion that marriage in accord with Nature's laws cannot be guided by any other principle. It links polygamy with divorce, and shuts its mind to the possibility of either, declaring them equal 'violations of natural law'. Whatever else may be challenged by the Church's critics, the view that marriage is for two people of opposite sexes has never been opposed by other than eccentric factions since the start of the Christian era.

To return, nevertheless, to what is continuously and most hotly attacked—the stubbornness of Rome in refusing to tolerate any form of divorce or artificial birth-limitation—the important question is whether *only* Roman Catholic marriages are made in Heaven? Let us ask it, with respect for the sayings of Christ as reported to us by the apostles.

* *Nullity of Marriage,* Sheed and Ward.

Do we honestly believe that God allows us complete freedom of choice, yet, once our selection of a mate has been made, locks, bolts and bars the door on our marriage bond?

It is part of Nature, i.e. of God's instrument, to infatuate those affected by young love. Often it blinds them to the inadequacies of their partner. The awakening to such imperfections can be both abrupt and long-delayed. It is never pleasant. Its result is frequently a desire to escape from what has become an unbearable relationship, but such escape is barred to all Roman Catholics.

Naturally this causes acute suffering. It is said to contribute to an unduly high suicide rate in some predominantly Catholic countries (though this may be attributable to other causes). There are other distressing statistics to be seen where the rule of Rome is applied most firmly, particularly in states which have adapted their laws to those of the Church.

In Italy, it was widely believed when the Divorce Bill was read in the Senate last year that at least one million couples were living together in mortal sin because, in the Church's eyes, they were not free to marry. In Britain, the United States, Ireland, and many South American countries, the unbending nature of the sacramental bond has brought similar evasions. For many involved, Catholics who have found themselves unable to live up to the rules of their God as interpreted by their Church, the twilight of such clandestine relationships is a constant source of anguish and remorse. For others, it is a daily tragedy separating them from the Church they once followed devoutly. In every case, it is a distressing result of what professes to be the application of a divine and loving will.

Thus it would seem that we are concerned with a state of marriage which is no more perfect than man himself, whatever the laws affecting it. There will always be disobedient Catholics, falling short of the high ideals of their

Church. No 'state of grace', such as that reflected by the sacrament of marriage, will prevent defection. Before accusing the Church of that responsibility, one should consider how comparatively rare such cases are.

In a world where divorce is daily more rife, and where self-indulgence grows hourly more evident and unashamed, the Catholics who toe the Roman line are an astonishing example of the power and splendour of their faith. As we know, the essential ties of these faithful Catholics to their Church are vested in the sacraments, of which marriage is one. What we will now take the liberty of testing—and somewhat more openly, perhaps, than is common in this secretive Church—is the strength and durability of the bond affecting the human spirit, and the human condition.

When Professor George Hayward Joyce, the Jesuit author of *Christian Marriage: an Historical and Doctrinal Study* wrote in 1933: 'Nature herself prescribes that the union of man and woman shall be an enduring association; that any condition of things in which such unions are temporary and terminable at pleasure is utterly repugnant to the constitution of human nature,' he was laying the keel for this enterprise. We shall examine what the courts of marriage secrets have to offer with as much forensic detachment as possible, but with strict regard for this Catholic view. The fundamental question is: should there, now, be change?

THREE

First Steps

It may have been Sophia Loren's boredom with administrative detail which kept the Ponti–Loren case out of the Catholic marriage courts—the actress was once reported as saying, 'I leave the birth and marriage certificates to the clerks.' Whatever the reason, their long and much-publicised struggle would seem to have been more easily resolved by a direct approach than by any other.

Perhaps it was that neither Carlo Ponti nor his wife Guiliana wanted to embroil the ecclesiastical courts in their situation. But Catholics are not in command of their law. It derives, says the Church, directly from God. It is the most carefully interpreted model of divine rule known to man.

Unlike the civil and criminal law of most western democratic countries canon law is utterly detached and aloof from the wishes of mankind. It was therefore of no importance than both Ponti and his wife, Guiliana Fiastri, wanted a dissolution of their marriage. Indeed Countess Fiastri's own actions and her readiness to sue for divorce, if such a divorce had been obtainable, were equally irrelevant.

What mattered before God were the facts of the case. Whether these, properly presented to the Rota, might have saved the three people involved one of the most tedious and anguished—not to say publicly lamented—ordeals in the history of the Church cannot be known. Certainly,

25

such a chance would seem to have existed in the early stages.

Why then were the most strenuous efforts in this direction not made by Carlo Ponti, a man of considerable influence and determination? The answer is hard to find. In Rome, Mrs Ponti told me she had struggled unsuccessfully for four years in the diocesan matrimonial courts, but their verdict had been adamantly negative: 'I am finished with it now,' she said. Also, we know from Sophia Loren's reported comments that the Pontis obtained only a legal separation. This did nothing, in the eyes of either the Church or the common law of Italy, to free them to marry again, and no decree of nullity has since been confirmed, to my knowledge.

An Italian lawyer who witnessed the drama in its early stages believes that there were personal reasons for Carlo Ponti's diffidence. It may have been that he truly believed (or was wrongly advised) that he could slip out of his marriage to Guiliana via the Mexican proxy courts. Many have shared this belief, and some have been successful.

Also it is a long and taxing ordeal to present a suit at the Sacred Rota. Indeed, at any of the marriage courts of the Church it is a most elaborate and often distressing business. One can understand and sympathise with anyone's wish to avoid such a process, and Ponti was a famous and busy man, much in the news. He had seen friends suffer both spiritual and material erosion through contact with the courts. This too we must not forget: he was deeply in love.

Carlo Ponti, I believe, chose the shortest route to what he hoped would be freedom to marry Sophia Loren because, at least temporarily, his heart ruled his head. If he had chosen the 'proper channels', he would have risked an unendurable delay while his suit was being heard in the lower courts, whatever country he had first presented it in. In Britain, there are twenty six Catholic dioceses of widely differing sizes. They share responsibility for at least advising nearly four and three quarter million British Roman Catholics on the complications of marriage. The diocesan bishops are responsible for the setting up and maintaining of tribunals to hear such cases, and primarily these courts must do so at what is called *first instance*.

Thereafter the procedure becomes more complicated, as cases approved by the *first instance* tribunal (that is to say granted an 'affirmative' verdict and regarded as having a fair chance of success) are sent for hearing a second time (*second instance*) on appeal. This is not an optional procedure, nor is it an appeal in the conventional sense. It is an obligatory safeguard for the lawyer-priests who administer God's law.

In plain terms, the appeal court has to double-check the reasoning of the lower court. If it cannot successfully dispute either its evidence or its law, the second court will return an equally affirmative verdict. If it succeeds, then it will bring in a negative. But to win a decree of nullity from Rome a petitioner must first have obtained two positive, or affirmative, verdicts in succession.

Courts of *first instance* are to be found in any suitable parish. *Second instance* courts are held in the metropolitan or provincial diocesan centres and their verdicts do not necessarily end a case, even when these agree with a lower court.

Should the petitioner lose at *first instance* may he not appeal directly to a higher court? Indeed he may; but if he succeeds at this *second instance* court, reversing the lower court's verdict, then his case must be heard by the highest court of all: Rome's Sacred Rota.

Since Catholics hold the sacrament of marriage as divine, no court on earth has power to set it permanently aside. The Rota may hear any petition claiming to have discovered proof that no marriage exists, which is the basis of all Catholic marriage cases, but as we know it cannot undo what God has done.

The Catholic marriage courts, therefore, are basically different from lay courts. In them, there is no need for cross-examination as it is understood at the British bar. Lawyers who argue cases before the Catholic courts are not seeking to prove one man's case against another; they are establishing fact.

For this reason the diocesan tribunals are small, and free of the emotional atmosphere of civil divorce courts. At Westminster, it was not uncommon until recently for the court to sit in a public waiting room of the Chancery, measuring only about twelve feet by ten feet. There is a far more commodious Hall of Sessions in the building, but this is considered unnecessarily formal, and seldom used. 'If the waiting room happens to be free,' a lawyer-priest explained, 'it is quite handy.'

Obviously, these courts are not trying to impress anyone. There are no robes and regalia, no wigs and gowns. A canon lawyer told me 'All questions and arguments are inquisitorial, rather than accusatorial.' What he wished to convey was that no attempt is made to put an appellant to the Church's matrimonial courts on trial. 'A Birkett or Marshall Hall would get nowhere' I was assured by the same advocate. He added: 'Since the clever extraction of facts by skilled examination in the witness box does not occur, it is the truth, not the individual, which stands trial in our courts.'

How does the ordinary Catholic, or indeed any other petitioner, find his way to these seats of divine justice? Assume for a moment that he has decided to seek an annulment. What would he do? First, he would go to his own priest for initial advice. It is possible that this spiritual guide would know a great deal about the ways of the courts; but if, as is more likely, he is ignorant on the subject he must pass his visitor on to someone more expert in canon law.

The potential petitioner will then be asked to go over, in detail, the events of his marriage as though it had happened only a day or so before. With infinite care the priest or lawyer will seek to establish good, valid reasons for suggesting that the marriage was not a marriage at all. Holding strictly to the truth, he will probe the most intimate and personal details of the marriage. But he will never willingly assist a couple who merely wish to see the end of an unwanted and tedious union. His role is to counsel, and to this end he will listen, and advise, asking questions from those who seek his help. Only when he believes there is a credible cause for a nullity plea will he advise in favour of a court hearing.

We must shortly consider what these causes are, and how they may be presented to the matrimonial courts. At this stage, it is only necessary to understand that the priest who first interviews a prospective candidate will ignore any other complaint, as well as all irrelevant pleas.

If the petitioner was to declare that he or she was the victim of desertion by a marriage partner, or infidelity, or mental or physical cruelty, the interviewer would be quite unable to help in ending the marriage. If the plea was based merely on the loss of love of a spouse, and desire for another union, this would be equally unsupportable. The courts are appointed by the Roman Catholic Church to be God's representatives on earth. They therefore have power only to deal with petitions which claim proof 'beyond all reasonable doubt' that no marriage exists, or has existed, between the couples involved. All other pleas are irrelevant.

Thus Catholic marriage courts need none of the awesome panoply of the law which stamps British civil and criminal courts. Their lawyers are not dressed and trained to represent dramatic amplifiers of a client's plea, indeed their knowledge and skills are brought into play only academically.

The judges, too, are fundamentally different from lay judges. These are not lawyers appointed to have authority over the disputes or misdemeanours of men. They hold the far superior position of being guardians of God's law, giving their approval only to suits which prove some basic failure to carry out the divine command. As we already know, mere failure of the course of the marriage or its harmony is not in this category. Only on matters concerning the fundamental structure, under which it should have been granted, can the holy sacrament be questioned.

Thus the privilege of being heard at *second instance* is reserved for those cases which are clear-cut, except in very rare and exceptional circumstances. The man or woman who insists on a second hearing, after an initial rejection, must have extraordinary perseverance, for in the lower courts everything possible will have been done. The petitioner, once he has approached the Church's tribunals, will have been assured of at least an intelligent and sympathetic hearing (how distressing this will be is another matter).

Little time is wasted on 'niceness', or ceremony, in these influential courts. Even the manner in which an ordinary Catholic comes before them is reduced to elemental informality. Usually, his only aid is the close link established previously with a local priest. If in good standing the appellant will already have admitted much, of what he now discusses, via the confidential medium of his Church's confessional.

In essence, doubts about the validity of the marriage in question must already be held, sincerely, by the priest. In many cases it is he who will have suggested that the case be brought on these grounds. The priest in the Catholic Church, as in other denominations, is both minister and moral adviser to his parishioners, and in marriage cases, he quite often has to become the family philosopher as well. Such intimate connection with the family does go some way towards easing the strain and embarrassment of sharing intimate matrimonial details, but a hearing is likely to be as humiliating an experience as any in the appellant's life.

At local level few priests know enough canon law to be more than generally helpful. They may have only the haziest picture of events as they occur inside the marriage courts. Their advice, when they venture it, is often weighted by misinformation and prejudice. Knowing how remote are the chances of a suit to the marriage courts being successful, they frequently deter those who might succeed.

But in theory, however frail the local priest's knowledge of the courts' machinery (especially of the highly secretive Sacred Rota in Rome), it should not prevent him from deciding whether or not an appellant has a case to plead. The priest's role is that of a pathfinder, instructed to guide all troubled feet in the right direction. Should he even suspect that a marriage was never truly made, then he will be bound to help set a case in motion.

The Roman Catholic with a marriage problem is now launched on a road which may take him all the way to Rome. Or, it may only involve him in considerable activity and anxiety at home for a long time. It will not be easy. He has every right, as a Catholic pilgrim, to present his case directly to the Vicariate Tribunal in Rome, and afterwards he may seek a Rotal decision at *second instance*. But the number of Catholics who do so is extremely small.

In common with all other large organisations, the Church of Rome prefers its petitioners to go through the normal channels. Thus the petitioner will be strongly advised to gather all possible evidence in support of his plea; and as much corroborating testimony, from as many witnesses, as possible. Then, with the aid of the priest, or canon lawyer introduced by him, he should be armed and ready to present the case before a diocesan court.

A qualified canon lawyer will now advise him. Almost certainly this attorney will be a member of the court, perhaps of the very tribunal of judges who may ultimately hear his case. To non-Catholic minds, this must seem odd, but it must again be remembered that none of the judges (in the sense that canon law uses the term) are, strictly speaking, judges of *men*. They are, as we have noted, merely interpreters of God's law as it applies to man.

Once it is believed by the Church that a genuine case exists, all efforts will be made both to present it and to help it on its way. At the same time every effort will still be made to disprove the plea, on the evidence supporting it, with all the vigour of those bearing responsibility for applying the will of God.

In the case of Carlo Ponti, we must assume he was advised that no reasonable case existed for him to present to the courts; otherwise he would hardly have chosen the easier, but ultimately useless, procedure of an ecclesiastical separation. No person so separated may marry again. Had there been the slightest chance of obtaining a decree of nullity, therefore, he would almost certainly have sought this.

In the preliminary stages of a case much depends on the enthusiasm shown by a petitioner's legal adviser. Only if this lawyer-priest believes, fundamentally, in the validity of the plea will he help the case along. Now begins the long and frequently harrowing business of seeking out necessary evidence; and of presenting it in the form required by the court.

Sworn statements should be made by all witnesses, before priests and, irrespective of where these individuals are situated, their testimony has to be obtained in writing. Additional testimonials are sought from experts, whose opinions can materially help the case, while doctors and surgeons may be asked to carry out examinations of the petitioner, or of his spouse: material evidence of this sort is of prime importance. It is the physical aspect of so many of these cases which has prompted the most critical questions about them. Absolutely no modesty is allowed to intrude between the truth and the tribunal, with frequently harrowing results; but it is claimed that these cannot be avoided.

A Catholic may present his own case, unrepresented by a canon lawyer, but to do so is no more popular in ecclesiastical than in civil courts. In the vast majority of cases, a Catholic legal advocate will represent the appellant before the marriage court, and he will normally be a canon lawyer, trained in the working performance of the Roman courts. He may, however, be a lay advocate. He must be a Catholic.

Only in extreme and rare instances can a non-Catholic lawyer present a case before the Church's tribunals. Indeed, such a lawyer would be most unlikely to know the complex points of law involved, or be able to bring the arguments to a point, and to present his case in a way likely to bring a positive verdict. Few lawyers outside the Church, and, fewer still non-Catholic lawyers, will take on such work.

Whoever does, is usually engaged to save expense, only when all evidence has been collected. Thus it may have taken months, even years, before the trial of truth begins. In very exceptional cases, at the direction of the court, the lawyer may remain present in the room during the interrogation of the appellant. But normally his function is confined—apart from guiding his client in canon law matters —to making a plea at the end of the hearing. Far from this being an opportunity for the customary melodramatics of civil court pleas, it calls for only a written thesis, and in this, the lawyer will argue his client's submission as tellingly as he can.

Again it may seem odd to non-Catholics that the court must insist on examining the appellant *in private*, without legal representation or guidance. But here the intimate nature of these matrimonial courts can clearly mislead. For it is at this point that the tribunal starts, so to speak, its true business as God's defender. It must now dig and delve for the absolute truth. Thereafter it must demand the most detailed corroboration and reiteration of all the statements which have been made.

That these have been written down, frequently, several months before the hearing, is of no consequence. The essence of this testing procedure is to tug separately and earnestly at every stitch in the assembled knitting. Any weakness that shows up will immediately unravel the whole design, and nobody need doubt that this procedure will be carried out to the last strand in the courts of the Roman Church.

With this in mind, let us examine the grounds which permit such luckless Catholics as appear before the courts, and their probing inquisitors, to hope for release from their unwanted marriage bonds.

FOUR

The Reasons Why

Four groups of causes exist by which a marriage may be proved null and void in the Catholic Church, but pleas need not be restricted to any one of them. A case before the courts can, often does, involve more than one; and if one fails, another may succeed.

Let us consider these causes. By their nature they are alien to non-Catholic thinking. Non-Catholics are used to divorce on such grounds as mental cruelty and desertion, but no such escape routes offer themselves here. In Catholic opinion, behaviour of this sort may make a marriage unbearable; it does not, and cannot, offer grounds for proving that it never took place. Catholic couples, therefore, face the prospect of having to endure a future of married separation, lasting for the rest of their time on earth. It seems a fate not too dissimilar to that of a Siamese twin whose partner has expired.

The first of the causes permitted as a reasonable ground for establishing nullity is described, simply, as: 'If the marriage agreed to was not a true marriage at all.' This does not necessarily imply that the priest who conducted the service was an impostor, or that the couple failed to say the right words in the right places during the ceremony; it can have far deeper implication.

Among Catholics, it is necessary only to show that *intention* to undertake true marriage was lacking. This, by itself, can produce strong evidence of nullity; so it is hardly surprising that this plea is frequently offered. But it must not be assumed that the mere statement of a previous frame of mind will be permitted to invalidate anything as sacred as the marriage bond.

What is required here, in unarguable and corroborated detail, is *evidence* of the failure of intention. Only where this can stand the rigorous tests of probes made into it by the lawyers of the courts will the judgement be favourable. But in such cases, once proved, the courts will allow that the marriage never truly happened.

This would be the case where a couple promised to wed, while one of them was secretly intending to withdraw from the marriage later on. So it would where one party had made a stipulation, preferably in writing, that no children should result from the marriage. Also, where something had prevented a marriage from becoming a full and complete union, likely to enjoy procreation. Such marriages would not be marriages, consequently God's sacrament had been withheld from them, and the courts would declare them null.

Of the three other, main grounds for proving a marriage void, the first is that the parties can be shown not to have been free to marry. Now this either means that they did not qualify for marriage at all, or that, for particular reasons, they *could not* marry each other. The difference between these is considerable.

Take a man who already has a wife alive. He wishes to marry another woman. He is 'not free' to marry the second woman, but there is no bar in general terms to his marrying. That is to say, in the theoretical circumstances which would exist if his marriage were proved null, he would be free.

If, on the other hand, the prospective husband was impotent, or under age, or in Holy Orders, or subject to solemn religious vows, then he would be totally ineligible to enter the marriage state. And if he should be a close blood-relation of the prospective bride, he would be prevented from marrying her, but not from marrying someone else.

Such blood relationship is known in the Church as consanguinity. It is frequently brought into dispute before the Catholic marriage courts, and it is complicated by the fact that this relationship need not exist directly. It can be introduced *through a previous marriage*, as was the case when King Henry VIII claimed nullity of his marriage to Catherine of Aragon on the grounds of her 'affinity'. Queen Catherine had previously been married to his deceased brother.

A consanguine union is expressly against divine law. But there are also cases forbidding marriage between individuals where public decency has been outraged. In certain cases, a married person's prior association with a close relative of his or her spouse will amount to this. Equally, where spiritual bonds have prevented an alliance (as between godparents and their spiritual children) the same bar exists.

Under this heading, also, we may find the far more common plea of mixed faith. This is to say that a Catholic and a *non-baptised* person have entered into a form of marriage, but it does not apply where both parties are baptised Christians; even if one is not a member of the Roman Catholic church.

On the face of it, one might assume that such a marriage was 'not a true marriage at all' (in other words, subject to the first 'causes' group). But this is not the case. The Roman Catholic party in such a marriage, should claim that he or she was 'not free' to marry the pagan partner. Only in that way does the hope of possible release lie.

One further ground exists under this heading, and it is

the most dramatic of all. The plea of 'crimen', by which is meant unlawful acts committed in order to pave the way to marriage, is a tragically popular one at the courts. Adultery, with the promise of marriage to the adulterous partner, may be held to be sufficient. So too, may the combination of adultery and the disposal by murder of the true marriage partner.

In fact, in such a case, adultery does not need to be proved, *nor even to have taken place*. It is sufficient to show that there was a promise of marriage to the other party at the time the murder of the true spouse was committed.

Finally, 'crimen' may be pleaded where one of the parties has been abducted by the other.

So we come to the third heading, or group of causes, eligible for a decree of nullity. It is where one or other of the parties to the marriage 'did not consent to the marriage'. They may have appeared willing at the time, even eager, but if insanity can be shown to have created a false state of mind, then the vows made will have no validity. Equally, where it can be proved that there was total ignorance of what marriage involved, in the mind of one or other of the parties, they cannot in the Church's eyes have made a true marriage. It is held that they were joined only in some inferior form of union which their deficient knowledge suggested.

Again (and there are historical cases of this) a person who marries by mistake cannot have consented to the marriage. The tragi-comic aspect notwithstanding, this is a reasonable cause for establishing nullity. And in certain countries where courting can be done by proxy, it is not as uncommon as one might imagine. When compared with this rarity, the use of force to make a person marry, and the consequent fear brought by this force, is quite common. Such marriages, of course, arouse widespread sympathy, and the Church shows great humanity in dealing with them.

Another cause which may prove a marriage null through 'lack of consent' is where a 'prior condition' was attached to the marriage. This is the most widely used of any, as a prospective escape-route, by the unscrupulous. It is quite a simple matter for such a condition to be laid down, even before the marriage is made, as a form of 'insurance'. This need not necessarily be used, or be expected to be used, but it provides a permanent means of ending the marriage if and when required, and it is another aspect of the reaction to the unbending and irrevocable nature of marriage vows which we will discuss in detail later on.

For the present, let us complete the causes under this heading. There is 'simulated consent' which really only means that the parties had no real intention of marrying properly, they only pretended to do so. This usually relies on evidence of false declarations, made by the couple before the wedding took place. Finally, there is where 'the proper form was not observed'; and in this last cause the subtle overlapping of Church and State law frequently adds to the general complexity. Catholic law has, since the Council of Trent in 1563, obeyed a decree known as '*Tametsi*'. In this it is declared that a marriage must be solemnised before a parish priest or his deputy *and two witnesses*. Where there are no witnesses, the marriage is clandestine, hence null.

In England, this did not apply until 1753, because 'common law marriage' was held to be legal here until then. Under the old common law marriage, any couple could agree to marry and simply *be* married, all that was needed was their mutual undertaking. When the Church first tried to stamp out this vague and undefined practice, a law was passed insisting that a priest should witness the marriage. But this was quickly found to be useless. A couple had only to shout their consenting oaths at each other, within a priest's hearing, and the deed was done. Even where a priest knew that it went against the Church, and possibly the State as well, there was nothing he could do about it.

In one notorious case, a young Frenchman named Gilbert Gaulmin dragged his priest out of bed to witness a wedding which must rank among the world's most bizarre. Both parties wanted it, but the priest was the unwilling attendant. They held him down on the floor of his bedroom while making vows of undying affection in his reluctant hearing.

There are other improper forms of marriage, which may equally be claimed as grounds for nullity, but mostly they deal with different aspects of the ceremony, service and procedure, and we need hardly list them here. In effect, wherever a marriage ceremony has been conducted in an irregular or unorthodox way there is likely to be a good cause for proving that no marriage exists.

We have now briefly outlined the means by which married Catholics may obtain release from unwanted bonds. Apart from the Pope's intervention, these are the sole causes acceptable in the marriage courts of the church. The crucial question in all of them is whether the sacrament of marriage was granted, or not. And, to weigh this delicate and holy matter, the finest legal brains of the Church apply themselves with unceasing vigour.

FIVE

Inside the Rota

Since 1941 the court of the Sacred Roman Rota has occupied a fifteenth-century architectural gem in the heart of urban Rome, about a mile from the Vatican. Known as the Chancery Palace, it stands in a quiet cul-de-sac on the left of the via del Corso, heading away from the Piazza Venezia. At first sight the yellow walls are unimpressive. A faded grandeur exists in the triple-tiered quadrangle, encasing as it does a succession of small columns supporting moorish arches. But this dominates a surprisingly drab courtyard, and one is hard put to it, at first, to equate this scene with the many guide-book references to the palace's 'quiet beauty'.

Only after long and thoughtful inspection do the rewards begin to emerge. Then, one notices the lyrical balance of design. As the spell deepens, the old building appears increasingly harmonious and unspoiled. On my first visit, I was surprised when a lift took me to the second floor and I was deposited beside a perspiring companion, an Italian lawyer with bulging brief-case, in what appeared to be a past century.

We walked into the cool, bare offices of the Sacred Rota. What had I expected? Remembering that this was the highest appeal court of the world's largest realm, one of the most powerful courts in the civilised world, and certainly the most secretive, my imagined picture had been of sombre richness. I had thought of solemn, regal trappings in the style of St Peter's during High Mass, a background as majestic as a papal ceremony. I had anticipated towering, Gothic heights and chill, pulpit-like seats of judgement. But what I saw was almost banal in its simplicity.

One's first impression is of offices and courtrooms which seem gaunt and uniformly plain. There are no rococo thrones, no elevated judgement seats (and, as far as I could see, no dungeons hid torture chambers!). At dark-stained, wooden desks (identical to those used by minor British civil servants) a handful of cassocked clerks sat at work in the outer Record Office. Directing them was a bright-eyed, happy, young Mexican priest, Father Pedro Lopez, who told me proudly that he was the first South American ever to have qualified as an *avvocato rotali*, one of the privileged seventy-five lawyers allowed to appear in person before the court. Additionally, Lopez had charge of several hundred dark-green, metal, file boxes lining the walls.

Some were labelled *sub secreto*. These, according to my guide, contained the cases for which there are few records and no published report; only verdicts. Without being able to take a full count, I would say that some eight to ten per cent of the total number of boxes were in this top-secret category, hidden from all prying eyes and publicity. What lay in those boxes will never, presumably, be revealed.

We moved into an adjoining room, Lopez showing the way. This was a communal chamber, equipped with a few desks and tables. Here, I was told, the nineteen judges of the Rota fulfil their more routine tasks. In low voices some of these dignitaries were talking among themselves. When later they met me, in interviews, they smoked cigarettes. Apparently there is no ban on smoking during their hours of duty. In all other ways these distinguished lawyers remain Catholic priests, who must abide by the strict rules of their Church.

As I nodded and smiled in acknowledgement of Lopez's kind but vain attempt to present me to these jurists—who seemed to have not a word of English between them—I could not help contrasting the scene with a robing room full of English justices. Anywhere but here, I realised, the dignity and bearing of such men would have stamped the atmosphere with aloofness. There would have been a sense of authority, a feeling of legal discipline and majesty. In contrast, these men were unaffectedly humble.

Once outside again, Father Lopez whispered that the room was used more than anything else as a common-room. Here the judges meet and compare notes. They use it to interview an occasional advocate, or caller, and to read notes and papers. They relax here, too, sometimes over a copy of *Osservatore Romano*, that bible in newspaper form of Vatican news and thought. It would be inhuman to suppose that they do not also gossip occasionally. These men are in intimate touch with some of the world's most intriguing secrets; eminent figures frequently confide in them. The rank, titles and riches of such people mean nothing when they enter this court, but their fame is known to those inside.

Though everyone who presents himself here comes as a humble pilgrim, seeking only to plead before God the cause of his marriage failure, yet these judicial witnesses would hardly be human if they did not find more than academic interest in the confidences of these celebrities. Roman Catholic priests, we know, are trained to exclude personal considerations from their thoughts while hearing confessions, but it is asking a lot to suppose that a Radziwill, a Rossellini, or any of the other hundreds of celebrities who have exposed their most intimate secrets here, can do so without causing a ripple of curiosity in the barren common room. I was not surprised to be told that, outside the court, the Rota judges are much in demand at the dinner tables of Rome's most discerning hostesses.

On the morning I was there, one of the judges grudgingly agreed to let me question him; but first I had to explain my purpose, and this was met with a considerable lack of sympathetic interest. Would a book do more than add to the deplorable sensationalism already heaped upon the court's proceedings? Was I in earnest? Was I a Catholic? Was I a lawyer? My answers to these and similar questions seemed to allay only a part of the obvious suspicion and disapproval which greeted my call.

Fortunately I had not gone to the Rota in hope of any more cordial reception, for warnings had reached me of its studied coolness towards outside enquiries. When I had been shown over the few rooms of the court, I realised that even in this I had been granted what was thought to be a rare privilege. Journalist friends in Rome later told me that only a handful of non-Catholics had ever seen inside the Rota, fewer still had been granted the chance of talking to the judge I was now with.

I should perhaps have been grateful that my host had at least agreed to see me. And, thinking this, I decided to try to dispel his distrust by urging that the ignorance of his court's procedure was causing widespread anguish. All this secrecy, I said, could only lead to false impressions. These were evident from the letters which, I had been told, regularly reached the court from bewildered Catholics, asking how much 'it would cost to get a divorce'.

At this, he grew a shade more tolerant. Not sufficiently to leave his shell completely; but he did talk more openly, and he answered many of my questions. Before I left him, my host begged me to keep his name out of anything I wrote. 'I am the equivalent of a British High Court Judge, and no publicity should be given to me on any account.

I will help you as far as I am able, *if you will promise not to mention my name.*'

Later I received a hint from one of his colleagues that professional caution might not have been the only reason for this reticence. Apparently any Rota judge whose name becomes public property immediately receives large quantities of correspondence. This comes from distressed, married Catholics who have never known before anyone by name to whom they might write. To attempt to deal with these pleas, tragic as they often were, without a secretary or a dictaphone to help him (often, too, unable to type enough to use one of the few typewriters), can so add to a judge's work that his few hours of relaxation are completely swallowed up. Anonymity is therefore a necessary form of protection.

We, on the other hand, are concerned here with lifting a veil of secrecy which has been strongly criticised inside and outside the Church in regard to this court. Hence, I propose to publish the names of those who, in the summer of 1967, were judges of the Sacred Rota. They were as follows (their countries and years of appointment to the Rota are alongside):—

Cardinal	Francis J Brennan (Dean)	USA	1940
,,	Bolesiao Filipiak	Poland	1947
,,	William Joseph Doheny	USA	1948
,,	Emanuele Bonet y Muixi	Spain	1950
,,	Giovanni Maria Pinna	Italy	1952
,,	Charles Lefebvre	France	1953
,,	Heinrich Ewers	Germany	1956
,,	Orvidio Bejan	Rumania	1956
Monsignor	Arturo De Jorio	Italy	1959
,,	Lucien Anne	Belgium	1959
,,	Gerard Maria Rogers	Scotland	1960
,,	Ernesto Fiore	Italy	1960
,,	Salvador Canais	Spain	1960
,,	Adamo Pucci	Italy	1961
,,	Guiseppe Palazzini	Italy	1961

Monsignor	Giovanni Abbo	Italy	1965
	Ugo Felice	Italy	1965
	Nicola Ferraro	Italy	
	Anton Czapla	Poland	

I was told they are an over-worked judiciary. 'It is an *extremely* onerous duty!' said one judge. He explained 'The number of cases is constantly growing. As the population of the world increases, people forget that this adds to our work. They have no idea how hard we work.' Perhaps we should therefore examine what the duties of the Rota are.

The court is principally involved, as we know, with marriage cases which have already received two conflicting verdicts in the lower courts; usually an affirmative followed by a negative. Where decisions by *first* and *second instance* tribunals have disagreed, the Rota can act as a court of *third instance*. Almost alone, it can make the casting decision. And from this there is afterwards no appeal, except in very rare instances (of which the Radziwill suit was one).

For cases arising in the greater part of the Western world, the ultimate decision lies with this Rota court of *third instance* in Rome. There is only one other: Spain has its own high appeal court. (Austria, in the time of the *concordat* alliance with the Vatican, had the same privilege, but this is no longer the case.)

During the Second World War the USA was also favoured with a similar dispensation. A court of *third instance* was set up for a three-year period, because of 'the difficulties of postal communication and the dangers occasioned by the war which is raging'. Since then there have been hints from the late Cardinal Spellman and others in the USA that the right to try cases on final appeal should be restored, and their supporters have pointed out that the growth of Catholicism in America is accelerating.

46

Indeed a present irony of the Roman Catholic Church is that while Italy leans more and more towards Communism (having added nearly a million votes to that party's strength in recent years), America is seeing the most rapid growth of Catholicism in the world; and this while the USA continues to have the most statistically shocking divorce rate. There are even those who forecast that the day will come when the Vatican will occupy a part of Boston, or some equally suitable American city, having been driven from Rome, no doubt, by heretical and Marxist jeers. But to return to our judges . . .

In operation, they must first read a volume of documentation sent up to them in which the lower courts will have rendered their findings. Fresh witnesses, and if possible new evidence, must now be obtained. All affidavits have to be re-sworn, for this final hearing, as a further safeguard. And a tribunal must be appointed.

The Rota judiciary is divided, for working and court purposes, into six groups of three judges. This does not include the Dean, though he will often take an active part. Hearings are taken in rotation by each of these groups. It is a sobering thought that work on every individual case may take *anything from one to ten years*!

Some two hundred verdicts are delivered every year by the Rota. This means that each of the tribunals has to deal with between thirty-three and thirty-four suits. It is a heavy burden, remembering the most complicated procedure involved. The judges are not allowed any modern aids, despite the wish of at least one recent American for the introduction of stenographic equipment. Reports must be written in Latin; and all other evidence must be presented in the language of its origin, a ruling which alone creates a vast burden of effort.

The work-load borne by the Rota is therefore certainly not over-rated. Cases of *third instance* are never simple, or they would not already have received conflicting verdicts. Thus the care and study required in dealing with them is often monumental. The question one feels impelled to ask is whether all this effort is justified by necessity?

Criticism of the court's slowness in this connection does tend to overlook many of the facts; it also leads, I found, to marked bitterness and sensitiveness among the judges. One of them scornfully told me: 'The diocesan courts accuse us of taking too long! Why, does the whole world think we just sit here, twiddling our thumbs? Far from it. In reality we get through an amazing amount of work.' On another occasion, the same judge commented: '*We* believe that the delays occur at the lower levels. Yet that is where there are supposed to be prescribed times for dealing with each case. In *first instance* it should be settled within two years. In *second instance*, one year.' The judge added: 'Our own consciences are entirely clear on the matter.'

Yet . . . yet . . . can the Rota escape all accusation of using time-wasting methods and processes? I do not think anyone who knows it would think so. In an age of space travel and satellite communications its methods seem quaintly archaic. During his time as Dean of the Rota, the softly spoken, white-headed Cardinal Francis J. Brennan of Philadelphia told me: 'There are measures for improvement which I should like to see adopted. For instance, if the code could include other languages instead of insisting that all other tongues must be translated into Italian or Latin, that would help to speed things up. It would also save costly delays. At present the judge has to take down all testimony in longhand, and although I have suggested using some form of stenography, they say it would cost a great deal. Italians, you know, don't just say a straight yes or no. I suppose it would cost about three hundred dollars, but that's all. It seems to me that some of the petitioners who come before this court could well afford to contribute more towards this if delays are so much resented.'

A recently appointed judge added: 'After all, they got themselves into it, didn't they? What they are asking here is an extraordinary service.' No doubt, but the Dean's impatience with the use of Latin was not universally shared. Among the other judges there were those who hotly defended it. 'Church Latin is such an *exact* language,' I was told. Also, 'Latin is universally understood. Our reports can be read anywhere in the world.'

The judge who said this held strong views on people outside Rome who accuse the court of sloth and secrecy. 'When people attack us,' he said, 'they forget how tedious this form of enquiry can be. They are pleading for reform, but I wonder how *they* would handle things? All this criticism is like rubbing salt in a wound. We lack space, money and time. What reforms can we make? There's talk of establishing Rotas in Germany and the United States, but I believe they'll have to keep to one central Rota. How else can one judge appeals without different—even faulty— interpretations of God's law creeping in?'

There must be a court of appeal inside the curia, the administrative governing body of the Church; and the Roman Rota does not deal exclusively with marriage cases. It is the high court of the Vatican State. In that capacity it hears cases of heresy, calumny and disputes over civil rights; yet marriage cases occupy ninety per cent of the agenda. Rota judges tend, therefore, to give far more time and thought to marital problems than to any others.

To outsiders it again seems strange, no doubt, that these nineteen celibates, with no experience of married life or the emotions and passions involved, should be set up to judge the most intimate aspects of sexual problems, and thereby to see more of them than anybody else in the world; but in Catholic eyes this creates no anomaly. A Roman Catholic obeys all laws, yet has allegiance to only one: that of his Church. If faithfully brought up from birth in the Church's ways, he will recognise that the lawyer-priest, in whose hands he may have to place his whole future happiness, is not limited because he lacks practical experience.

As Christ was celibate, so the Church interprets God's wish in the direction of its own 'fathers'. They are on a higher and more virtuous plane than can be reached via marriage and procreation. The act of celibacy, the voluntary renunciation of the sins of the flesh and their pleasures, is a higher and more glorious aim.

Hence, the Church sees marriage as a God-given institution raised to the level of a sacrament, but not as the highest and most virtuous form of life. And the Rota judges can participate in some of the most delicate arguments, touching on all possible physical aspects (even to exact biological measurements) of a marriage, while remaining spiritually aloof.

The role of judge at the Sacred Rota is one of high honour in the Church, and the curia is rich and powerful. But the amount of money spent on the court is perhaps the most carefully-guarded of all its secrets. I asked several officials and judges what it was, and they fobbed me off with vague replies. The Church, I was told, has enormous expenses in many directions. There can never be enough cash in its coffers to provide what civil courts outside 'would be sure to squander' on similar cases. Shortage of money may restrict the court, both in the time taken over hearings and in the methods used, but this is not always considered a bad thing.

'We don't want to give the impression that it is a simple and speedy matter to obtain judgement in a nullity suit,' I was told. 'Nor do we wish to lose the sense of mystery. Our reports of cases are *intentionally* wrapped in this. After all, this is not a place of entertainment for the salacious.'

Similar utterances could be heard from several other judges, who obviously resented the inquisitiveness of the heretical world outside. It did seem that experience in recent cases, where the court had been badly scorched by publicity, had left a deep scar; and when I went to the Rota to interview the Dean for the first time I had this very much in mind. His courteous but rather testy manner confirmed my view.

Thus, when I led our conversation towards this recent criticism of the court, I was sharply rebuked. The Rota was an august, diligent body, I was informed. It had no time to concern itself with mere speculation. What outsiders said of it could be of no possible consequence, etc. etc.

Yet the Dean seemed to me to reveal the core of frustration and resentment felt by these judges. As we discussed the recent Radziwill case, he told me: 'People talk, they don't know. They don't begin to know the facts before they give utterance to their thoughts.'

Another judge was even more scornful of outside attitudes: 'There are so many false beliefs,' he said. 'In Scotland, people still think that all the pubs are owned by the Catholic Church! There is tremendous ignorance of what we are doing, which is simply upholding God's laws. The result is a distorted picture.'

To say that the blame for this can only lie in Rome, where the conventional curtain of secrecy and suppression is draped over the ancient courts of the Rota, with its *sub secreto* files and vows of silence, is hardly to court favour. I repeatedly suggested to the judges I talked to that the effect of removing secrecy would be an almost miraculous clearing of suspicion and ignorance. Nobody was prepared to accept this.

Cardinal Brennan did say he was human enough to wish sometimes that the rules were other than they are. 'There are so many tragic cases where we should like to be able to help,' he said, 'but the way is not open.' Here, in the heart of the Church's highest court, one might have hoped to hear more positive views.

If change and improvement is needed to reanimate this ancient court, this is where it should start. Yet every suggestion that the judges might take a hand in any such spring-cleaning was met with disdain. 'We are not here to question what we do,' was the stock reply to my enquiries.

Where my queries touched on the validity of the Church's interpretations of God's commands, I also encountered a marked evasiveness. Time and again I was told that my questions were 'too pastoral', or that they should be referred to theologians rather than to practising lawyers. The impression left on an enquiring mind is inevitably one of inhibition and resentment.

It must, I think, be bluntly said that if nobody will accept the responsibility for re-appraisal of these interpretations and customs, then the image will continue as it is for a long time to come; and unless one can believe that the succession of pontiffs in Rome has each received direct communication from God on the subject, then it must be faced that the last reported utterance of God on these matters occurred in Jesus Christ's lifetime nearly two thousand years ago. Is there, I asked, no possibility of doubt that a change may have become necessary since then? Can these ancient interpretations still suit a world which has outgrown almost every one of its earlier beliefs, and which is now challenging the frontiers of life, death and the universe? Such enforced changes as Rome has allowed itself during the present century argue otherwise.

The Rota began as an extension of the Apostolic Chancery. It was originally entrusted with the preparation of causes for marriages to be declared null. Exactly when it was started, by what pope or curia, is a matter of opinion. It was certainly Innocent III who gave it power to pass sentence. And after Gregory X the chaplains were permitted to form a permanent tribunal. Pope John XXII assigned them permanent quarters, and, in 1331, re-organised their powers and procedures. In the following century, Sixtus V fixed the number of chaplains-auditors, as the judges were known, at twelve. Later, in 1747, Benedict XIV definitively determined the jurisdiction of the tribunal through his *Constitutio Justitiae et Pacis*.

By all this it can be seen that the court had no easy birth. Its whole history has been so beset by reformers that any irritation it shows towards suggested change today can at least be understood. Under Pope Gregory XVI (1834) the Rota was again enlarged to act as the Tribunal of Appeal for the Papal States. Then, in 1870, its activity and power almost disappeared. For the rest of that century, and for the first eight years of the next, it slept in a sort of suspended animation; not dead, but lacking all outward power.

On 29th June 1908, the court was re-awakened. It was restored to full power by St Pius X in his *Constitutio Sapienti Consilio*. For more than a half century since that important turning-point it has worked steadily at the arduous, highly responsible task of testing the bonds of holy matrimony.

Its name, the Sacred Rota or 'sacred wheel', leads to questions about its origin. A distinguished journalist and writer, Corrado Pallenberg, has suggested four possible answers. In his book *The Vatican From Within* (Harrap), Pallenberg explains that quite probably the auditors sat in a circle, or that cases were considered in rotation; or that an ancient, porphyry wheel was once embedded in the centre of the floor where the court met; finally, because of a revolving, wooden bookcase in which the law codes were housed.

I could find no support for these notions. My informants believe that the Rota was simply the form taken in judging certain cases, where the papers of these were rotated round a table at which all judges sat. The practice still continues, occasionally, today. But when a suit proves exceptionally difficult, or the appointed tribunal fails to reach agreement, the Dean can command all the judges to meet *omnibus videntibus*, 'with all seeing'. Then, they occupy the largest room in the palace. I was shown it, situated at the end of a lofty corridor, the figure eight above its oaken doors.

Inside I saw a huge rectangular chamber, scarcely less bare than those of the outer offices, but containing a long wooden table around which were placed nineteen chairs. Before each place was a clean blotter, together with ruled foolscap notepaper, overprinted with the cypher of the Sacred Rota.

I lifted a sheet of this from the table, and studied the unusual crest: a solid circle, or wheel, marked with the positions of the hours; inset, a symbolic bird; a halo round its head, its wings spread, apparently, in supplication. No one knows when this crest first came into being, or why.

Tall windows of leaded panes let a pale light filter into the room. When Roman skies are dull, I was told, it can be supplemented by three hanging electric chandeliers, which cast a shimmering reflection on the glazed fronts of tall bookcases set against the walls of the chamber. The only warmth in the room stemmed from the colours of papal portraits, dominated by a rather sour painting of Pius XII by A. Pontrandolfi, dated 1942. In crimson robes, this occupied the central position of the windowed, far wall.

Here, in Room Eight, the most weighty decisions of the Rota are made. I am told that the *omnibus videntibus* procedure is remarkable. The assembled judges separate into their groups of three, then they are required to offer their verdicts in turn on the suit under consideration. When any two concordant decisions are given, the case is closed. But if each verdict reverses the last, it is theoretically possible for a case to go the rounds indefinitely. Whether or not any case has ever exceeded one complete revolution I was unable to discover, but my guide thought it unlikely. Taking into consideration the frequent reversals incurred in many of the marriage court decisions through the various *instances*, I should have thought otherwise.

Merely by looking at this empty room, it is possible to imagine the controversial secrets locked in its walls; to sense the human anguish, hope and despair in the tragedies which have been revealed at the innocent-seeming table. The silent pontiffs in their frames could tell much, though now not a speck of incriminating dust remains. But the record, censored though it is, is worth consideration; as are the vivid stories of those who have bared their closest secrets in Room Eight.

SIX

Inquisition

To witnesses expecting an assault on their privacy as individuals, the marriage courts may not seem harsh and offensive. But, by the very nakedness of their approach to intimate details in the loves and lives of their petitioners, they can have little regard for modesty. Indeed, they flaunt all conventional delicacy; and the questions asked by Rota judges, all sworn celibates with no personal experience of married life, are penetrating. They probe to the root. Everything relevant to their searching and highly detailed enquiries is ferreted out ruthlessly. In pursuit of absolute truth, no holds are barred. By going repeatedly over the same questions and answers they endeavour to trap the unwary liar. Expert evidence is brought to test the validity of all specialised testimony and often, by a deliberate technique, the judges allow time to drag with the aim of making it hard for witnesses to remember what they said previously.

Thus the experience of giving evidence in support of a nullity petition at the Rota can involve a gruelling 'confessional' of intimate marriage secrets. It does not, and cannot, become a forensic encounter between acidulous lawyers. It is an inquisition and not a cross-examination. There is only truth at stake.

The reputation of this secretive court is often coloured by emotional gossip, but in Rome it is regarded with almost medieval awe. Women with personal experiences of the Rota talk of terrifying, humiliating and heart-sickening experiences. Many report a sense of outrage and shock which seems barely credible. A woman who has lived through a difficult and unhappy marriage is unlikely to be so squeamish that her feelings can be lightly shocked. But there seems to be a tradition for a woman, on returning from the court, to show off her wounds.

Yet not all petitioners exaggerate. The inquisition they must endure does go to astonishing lengths. Some of the questions asked might, as a Rome reporter commented, 'shock a call-girl'. Nothing is too intimate or sacred for the judges' ears. Indeed, much of the evidence is suitable for reproduction in medical and legal textbooks only (were it ever reported fully, which it is not).

The celibate fathers may ask a young wife to describe *in detail* acts of physical love she has shared with her husband. She may be pressed to define her exact feelings at such times, even to the clinical measurements and methods where these illuminate some specialised point. If a woman claims she never intended to have children, as many do, she will almost certainly be subjected to such analyses. Presumably, these are to test the strength of her conscious as well as her sub-conscious feelings.

Just as commonly, a petitioner will allege she never intended her marriage to last. The Rota will then demand repeated assurances that her acts of love were no more than self-indulgence. If pride allows her to reply 'no' to this, then her case will be seriously weakened. The inquisition of the marriage courts is a stern trial of humility.

From the shortened reports of some cases, published in Latin a discreet ten years afterwards, it is clear that the way a question is answered is often as important to the outcome as the answer itself. Rota judges must seek to establish the whole picture of a marriage, striving to follow its course from beginning to end. The enquiry therefore ranges over every aspect of the union, even the merest tiffs, which may have disturbed it. But the court is concerned, not with the salacious and titillating exterior, but with the inner relevance of what is said. When the judges probe, they do so in the interests of spiritual justice. On trial before them is the sacrament of marriage.

It is pointless to deny that the secrets locked in the plain, distempered walls of the Rota courtrooms are among the world's most delicate. The excuse is that this court is responsible not merely to man, but to God. And before Him there need be no reluctance to expose intimacy. Nothing is therefore taken on trust, and testimony, however harrowing, cannot be accepted until corroborated and cross-checked. But is it not surprising that cases of this sort grind on for year after year?

The same questions have to be asked, time and again, of the same witnesses. Discrepancies in answers are most carefully noted; no lawyers are allowed in the court with their clients to help guide faltering tongues and memories. Yet many Catholics commend this form of inquisition. They support it in the belief that anything less searching would encourage lies and cheating. And, of course, one can respect their views; but it would be more to the point if those who have actually suffered the experience of facing the Rota were to speak well of it.

One young man who had won a nullity decree at the court did, in fact, give approval of its methods when I talked to him. But he refused to allow me to publish his name, and he was the only supporter I could find among those who have appeared as witnesses. What this enthusiastic petitioner said was: 'There is nothing at all to fear. Provided you have made a serious, well-defined and scrupulously honest presentation of your case, all will be well. The essential is a really sound lawyer. He must know how to put arguments in a way the court understands. It is no use women coming to the court, as they do, relying on a friend as witness. Probably they will only tell the court a lot of rubbish. It is pointless for them to come, just as it is meaningless for those who do not understand the true function of the court to approach it at all.'

This man continued: 'Foreigners, especially, are guilty of coming to the Rota seeking divorce, rather than nullity. They offer evidence that "we quarrel" or "we throw plates at one another". Such details of their life together are, of course, a complete waste of time, and the court's temper naturally sharpens as a result; judges are only human. But if someone presents an honest, sincere and valid case he will not be asked to face an inquisition. The facts will speak for themselves. When people complain that they have been harshly treated, they should remember they have been the instrument of their own torture. The judges want only two things: a correct case, and proof. Provided they get them, there will be very little unpleasantness. If they do not, then in my experience it is the petitioner who is to blame, not the court.'

He told me he had appeared before the Rota four or five times, and had faced the three judges and answered their most frank and intimate questions; the Defender of the Bond, the advocate charged with destroying all fallacious evidence, had interrogated him fully. Yet he had remained unshaken.

Of the Defender of the Bond's inquisition, he said: 'His questions were very direct and pertinent, never aggressive. I know it is said that he sometimes puts deliberately ruthless and embarrassing questions, but that was not my experience. I think that that sort of thing happens only when the person concerned brings up a particularly delicate matter himself. I certainly saw no evidence of anything frightening. One must, of course, try to be as normal as possible.

But the court seemed to me to do their best to put me at ease and make me feel relaxed.'

On the same note, he continued: 'Sincerity is all-important. The Rota does not like people who come cynically before it. If the cases are simple, they are usually sincere, and that is what the court likes. I found them very understanding indeed. One can say that it is entirely a question of integrity and common-sense on the part of the petitioner how he or she gets on, but the method of inquisition, rather than cross-examination, *can* trick the unwary. It gives a lot of rope to those who are not telling the truth. I myself never re-read what I had previously told the court when I appeared at a later hearing to answer similar questions. I'm sure that that impressed them, because they knew I was speaking from my heart, and telling the truth.'

In the face of such a tribute as this, it may seem impertinent to press for further elucidation. But not all complaint of oppression by the courts is biased or malicious. Other petitioners insist that a strong element of callousness attaches to the questions and behaviour of the judges, especially when interrogating sensitive, young women. It would be surprising, of course, if any court of law was not subject to similar criticism from time to time, but the Rota is protected from public gaze by secrecy and vows of secrecy. If malpractices do develop, they develop unseen.

And here the judges are priests. They are sworn to help the spiritually ailing, to encourage the weak. In certain cases where women have experienced their legal behaviour it has seemed curiously at odds with such principles.

There is a tragic instance I came across of a titled Italian woman, still bitter and upset fifteen years after her encounter with the Rota. This woman now has many intelligent and sensitive friends in the country where she has taken refuge, and she is far from being obsessed by her ordeal. Indeed, she leads an apparently normal, healthy and full life. But her story, as she told it to me, is harrowing enough to have permanently disturbed many women.

In 1947, this Countess ended a three-year struggle to convince the Rota that her marriage had not been a true bond, as she had innocently married a man related to her by blood, a second cousin. She was subjected, she told me, to 'torture, real torture'. In her own words, 'I was in and out of the court-room for a whole year. I must have been summoned to appear at least fifty times. I had begun to lose hope.'

The Countess continued: 'Like all people who seek annulment, I had to appear alone, without even my lawyer. He had presented my case, but was never allowed to be in court with me. I had to go to that huge, gaunt building alone to face a cluster of old men seated round a wooden table. I was allowed to sit down, facing a crucifix on the plain wall behind the central judge. When the hearings began, nobody told me they would go on for as long as they did. Nobody told me anything. I was told that I might be kept for an hour, or a week; it depended on the wishes of the court. I remember looking at the small, high window, rather like a prisoner, wondering how long it would be before I was released.'

The Countess shivered at the recollection. Then she went on with her description of the procedure of the court. She said: 'You are summoned to appear at times arranged by the tribunal. They never let you know when these times will be. As for your dress, you may wear what you choose. But you are not allowed to smoke. Although there is no apparent formality, the atmosphere is sinister. A judge sits facing you. He mutters Latin under his breath, and asks his questions in a grumbling, querulous tone. With me, he spoke his own language, Italian. Whatever he said and I answered was written down—in longhand on lined, fools-cap paper—by a notary who sits on the judge's left. Those questions went on day after day. We went back and forth over the same ground. I knew that they were trying to trick me, to get me to say the opposite of what I had said before. There was no matter, however intimate or distressing to me, which was not probed into and gone over, again and again.'

Later, she recalled: 'There were no guards, so far as I know. No locked doors. But the feeling I had was of being in a terrible prison. By the time my case was finished I was a nervous wreck. The Defender of the Bond had become a sort of spectre. I woke up terrified after seeing his face in my dreams. *He* was the worst! He seemed to wait until I was exhausted or distressed before starting his inquisition. I was sitting on a hard chair, wretchedly uncomfortable, and sometimes I wanted to get up and run out of the room. He frightened me. But at first I had no idea how dangerous he was. Then, one day as we adjourned for lunch, he came over and began a cordial conversation. It was all about my family. In particular he seemed interested in my father. He said he had heard that my father kept a very fine collection of cigars. He was very partial to a good cigar himself. Couldn't my father spare him one or two? The question was put in a half-joking manner. But after the strain of his examination, and the terror of that room, I babbled: "Of course, I'm sure he could. Let me bring you a box." After lunch I looked across at him. There was no sign of warmth of recognition in his eyes. He was back in his role as what I always thought of as *l'avocatto del diavolo*—the devil's advocate. Then he rose and told the court that I had offered to bribe him with some cigars before lunch. I was admonished. Very soon afterwards he again switched his manner. He could be utterly charming when he wanted to be. The way in which he changed from one mood to the other reminded me of stories I had read of brain-washing. *It was absolute Third Degree!*'

Nevertheless the poor Countess was successful. Her annulment was finally granted, and she is no longer encumbered by an unwanted marriage. Indeed her 'torture', as she described it, had been worthwhile—unless one counts the cost to her faith. This woman has a child. She is now deeply concerned about the child's status on earth as well as its spiritual standing. 'I can't feel my daughter really belongs to me,' she said. 'My marriage did not take place, so how can I have had a child by it?'

Such fears are groundless. The children of putative, or supposed, marriages are no different in law or standing from any other legitimate offspring of a marriage. But apprehensions are natural in a woman who has undergone a major psychological ordeal.

In fact the Rota is always more lenient—where the law allows it to be—in cases where a large number of children of a marriage exist. Unfortunately the Countess was not to know this. She and others like her bear away scars of fright and ignorance, both of which might easily be alleviated.

The young English impresario, David Pelham, provides another viewpoint on the marriage courts. A Protestant, he approached them to try to establish the nullity of his previous marriage. The reason was that he wanted to marry again, and the girl was an Italian Roman Catholic. Pelham knew that his previous wife's first husband had been alive when she married him, giving grounds under Catholic law for annulment.

To say that he found the courts tiresome is to put it mildly. 'It was a straightforward case,' he explained, 'but the time it was made to take was fantastic. Months. Meanwhile the girl I wanted to marry could have been desperately anxious to wed. She could have been pregnant. She could have died. It's pretty heartless, isn't it?'

To a sophisticated Protestant, it unquestionably is. But the Catholic flock does not, as a rule, suffer from oversophistication. It largely accepts that the ways of the Church, even if they appear strange and sometimes harsh, are none the less the ways required by God. They reason that the Catholic Church was appointed by Jesus Christ to bring these ways into the world, and its methods of fulfilling this mandate must be God-given also. Even to question it approaches heresy.

In Rome, another young Catholic woman described to me her dealings with the Rota, and these clearly showed that she, too, had suffered deeply from the court's inquisition. She was an attractive young executive in one of Italy's booming commercial firms. Her mind, despite the ordeal, was obviously both lively and intelligent, but her opinion of the Rota was unshakeable. It was, she said: 'most unnecessarily awful'.

'Although I was young,' she said, 'and with very little experience of life, they asked me *terrible* questions. I remember feeling completely shattered by it all, especially since I had still not recovered from the failure of my marriage and its consequences.'

This woman had practically no money, and the costs and worries of her case seemed to her to have, as she put it: 'plunged my whole world into darkness'. She said: 'The Rota couldn't have cared less if I was upset. The judge sat there smoking a big pipe. He kept prowling round the place where I sat, puffing out clouds of smoke. I was kept there for hours, with no knowledge of how long I would have to stay. The hearings just went on and on. On one occasion I was subjected to this inquisition for six hours on end without a break!'

In her youth, she told me, she had been a member of her university Communist party. When, during her hearing at the Rota, she asked if she could have some lunch, or refreshment, the Defender of the Bond commented sarcastically: 'I thought Communists didn't get hungry.' She was soon to learn that this was more than rudeness, it was also an attack on her nullity petition.

When she had married, she claimed, she had still been a Communist and for this reason had not believed in lasting marriage. In nine cases out of ten, especially where the petitioner has written Communist literature attacking Catholic belief in marriage, this plea works. Here, the Defender of the Bond was deliberately challenging her evidence.

This woman also won her case but, as there is no right of access to the full Rotal court reports, it is not possible to check how deeply she suffered during the trial. Judges and lawyers of the Sacred Rota are not unanimous about how severe these ordeals are. Had these informants exaggerated the terrors of their inquisition? Was the Defender of the Bond, in particular, slandered by these remembered horrors? An experienced judge told me: 'It's all nonsense. Of course we have to ask questions. But we are never merciless or heartless. After all, this is a court of law. It is our duty to get at the truth. But it is simply not true that we probe into people's souls, or anything like that. There is no cross-examination here, remember. We are not setting one individual up to triumph over another. Our enquiries are restricted to question and answer, and to sworn evidence and testimony.'

In contrast, a distinguished Catholic theologian told me in London: 'Sometimes it can seem that the Rota has no heart. The delays are terrible. They appear unduly cruel to those kept waiting. I believe that many canon lawyers and priests have no idea of the suffering caused, any more than the perpetrators of the Inquisition in Spain had. They, too, thought it was all for the good of man's eternal soul.'

It is as well to note these opposing views before we pass on. They may suggest that those highly placed within the Church are not always in touch with sane, ordinary views outside. One of the most distinguished of the seventy-five Rota lawyers, Professor Fernando Della Rocca, said in Rome that 'Any suggestion of inhumanity by the courts I deeply resent.' But he, too, may be over-shadowed by the persuasive atmosphere of the Vatican. In more detail, he said with feeling:

'A matter of faith is involved here, not merely a question of man's rights or wrongs. Sometimes in these cases of a soul the ultimate object is the salvation, and we lawyers know that we are in a very heavily responsible position. Advocates like myself who represent petitioners, yet have studied the law of the Church, find ourselves permanently placed between the judge and the poor petitioner. Often we see our clients complicating their cases by their own actions, and this can lead to a great deal more inquisition than would otherwise be necessary. Perhaps they have gone outside the Church in their impatience to divorce and re-marry. When they come to us and ask for the matter to be settled for them, it is not always so easy. I know that these are the cases which the judges like least of all.'

The terms of reference given to the tribunals by successive pontiffs have always taken account of this failing. When Pius XII delivered an important address to the assembled Rota judges in October 1941 he amplified these terms, with a clarity and precision seldom found in ecclesiastical speeches. The wartime Pope said: 'Everyone knows that the Church is rather wary and disinclined to favour them (nullities). Indeed, if the tranquility, stability and security of human intercourse in general demand that contracts be not lightly set aside, this is still more true of a contract of such importance as marriage.

'Here firmness and stability are necessary for the common welfare of human society, as well as for the private good of the parties and their children. And here too sacramental dignity forbids that it be lightly exposed to the danger of

66

profanation. Everyone knows that human hearts are too much inclined—for this or that grievance, because of disagreement with or weariness of the other party, or in order to pave the way for union with some other person who is the object of a sinful affection—to seek freedom from the bond of marriage already contracted. Hence the ecclesiastical judge must not show himself ready to declare the nullity of marriage. But he should rather make every effort to contrive that what has been invalidly contracted be validated . . .'

Later, the Pope continued: 'In case validation of the marriage is impossible . . . or because the parties refuse to give or to renew their consent, a judgement of nullity cannot be refused to a party who seeks it justly . . . Provided the alleged invalidity be established with that *certainty* which in human affairs is called *moral* certainty. That is certainty which excludes all prudent doubt, being based on positive reasons.'

The Pope concluded with particular reference to recommendations for dissolution of marriage: 'Finally, as regards the dissolution of the bond of a marriage validly contracted. The Rota is called upon to investigate also in such cases whether all the conditions are fulfilled which are prerequisite . . . so that the recommendation can be made to the Supreme Pontiff for the granting of that favour.

'The ecclesiastical judge is called upon to determine whether the existence of these prerequisite conditions is sufficiently established . . . this investigation must be conducted with all severity, rigour and diligence. The more so since there is a question of a vicarious power in a matter of divine law . . . It is true that in our times, in which the disregard for and carelessness of religion have revived the spirit of a new pleasure-seeking and proud paganism, there is in many places a sort of mania for divorce. Such as would dissolve marriages more easily and lightly than leasing and hiring. But this inconsiderate mania is itself unworthy of consideration. . . .'

We are left in no doubt by these words. 'Severity, rigour and diligence' are not mild instruments. They can be applied only with firmness and determination, even at the cost of personal and human feelings. The trained lawyers who have thus been instructed will know that their duty lies along a stern path. Any weakness or softness on their parts can bring collapse dangerously close.

SEVEN

Corruption

Turn now to a side of the marriage courts which, more than most, has stained their image: the cost. Tragic petitioners to these courts have been reportedly ruined by spending fortunes on innumerable ecclesiastical lawyers, hearings and procedure. Are these stories true and, if so, can the high charges be justified?

The Catholic Church has the highest possible ethics in the matter of charges made in its name. Indeed more than half the cases brought to the Rota in Rome are paid for entirely from its coffers. But the Church may offer help or encouragement only to those who, it believes, stand a fair chance of winning their cases. Where less than reasonable doubt exists, no honest priest, canon lawyer or Rotal advocate will accept a brief for a nullity case. In these cases, lay lawyers (barred from practising at the Rota itself, but free to offer their services as professional 'guides' to a petitioner on the outskirts) are temptingly available; and costly.

Advocates of the Church may be forced by training and conscience to reject a case. The 'guide' lawyers can and do offer at least a few grains of hope. Their knowledge of ecclesiastical law and its more practicable areas can be bought by anyone. But, once involved with them, a client may find himself spun upwards in a spiral of fees and expenses. 'Guide lawyers' do not as a rule work alone, they operate as links in an increasingly expensive chain.

So the first of them will probably profess much and do little. Nevertheless, before the client's patience evaporates, the lawyer will discover just the man for this or that particular point. Later, another complexity will provide the most urgent need for guide number three. And so on.

Between them, these associated grafters can play along a bemused and anxious client until either his temper or his resources have been exhausted; yet there is always just the chance that they may, in fact, succeed in winning the case.

It happens in this way. The majority of lay lawyers who work on Roman Catholic matrimonial cases are both fair in their financial demands and scrupulous. But the few who are more interested in the end product—the winning of a nullity decree—than of any ethics concerned, use a variety of tricks. Their fees can be astronomical. There is no guarantee of their success, even where they stoop to the use of perjured witnesses and other means. Everything will depend on the size and suitability of the loophole through which their client's case is to be driven.

It is these professional exploiters who are responsible for the many tales (some of which I have checked and found to be tragically exact) of exorbitant charges, in cases which have lingered on for years without ever reaching the Rota. Those who have true and simple grounds for proving their marriage null are unlikely to become their victims, because strong cases are advised and assisted from the outset, either by priest or Church. It is only when a good Catholic finds himself in a bad marriage, perhaps in an impossible alliance, that he will pay to get out.

The lawyer who at this point encourages a client to continue a case with almost no hope of gaining a favourable judgement is the worst sort of rogue. Similarly a lawyer who persuades his client to commit perjury in order to gain a nullity decree is guilty of a criminal act. Nevertheless there are plenty of both in Rome. Some cynically accept cases, and fees, with no realistic expectation of success. Others are plain crooks whose fees are higher, but whose contrived cases, I am told, are far more likely to be successful.

Before going to Rome I had heard of these rogue advocates who claim to know 'ways and means' by which unscrupulous annulments can be obtained in the Catholic Church. In the shadow of the Vatican, often with surprising ease, I was able to meet more than one of them. We had long and intimate discussions. They outlined the deceptions and frauds used. I heard their boast that a number of nullity decrees had been won for Catholics who 'would have had absolutely no chance' if they had not been dealt with by their methods.

There was one particularly candid rogue whose practice, he admitted, depended on open abuse of the law he had sworn to uphold. To me, he made no bones about the methods which he and apparently others employ. These, he said, involved the forgery of documents, and persuasion of witnesses to commit perjury. His moral, if not ethical, justification was a belief that those who suffer have a right to mercy. His argument was that the Church was entirely to blame for his clients' suffering. In support, he claimed to have 'infallible knowledge' of relevant cases where Catholics had been told by their priests and canon lawyers that no help could be offered to them. 'With some,' he said, 'it was a sentence of living death.'

The most alarming of this man's assertions was the extent of the corruption in marriage cases brought before the Catholic diocesan courts, and the Rota. In Italy there are some three hundred dioceses, each of which once had its own separate court. These were later replaced by nineteen regional courts, due to the failure of some of the smaller dioceses to produce reliable and competent judges. But there are still two thousand or so cases heard by them annually, giving the lawyers of the country plenty of scope for their activities.

My informant assured me: 'I would say that nine hundred and fifty five out of a thousand of these cases are completely faked.' If only fractionally true, this is a scandalous assertion. That such wholesale corruption is possible, against a code of rigid law which has been practised by skilled and exhaustively-trained lawyers for centuries, is astonishing.

A judge of the Rota told me he was 'well aware' of the temptations for witnesses to commit perjury. Could the judge have had any idea of the depths of corruption suggested by this figure? Almost certainly not. Yet one of his colleagues lamented to me on another occasion about the disgraceful charges of the civil lawyers who 'feast on the unwary'.

This judge complained: 'If only people could see how they can be taken for a ride by these practitioners!' The statement could more aptly have been made to the marriage courts themselves. Has the Rota any idea how many times *it* is being taken for a ride by the same lawyers? Corruption in Rome and around the marriage courts is believed by those shielded by the Church to be far further away from their skirts than it actually is, and such a question would probably have been met with scorn. 'We are constantly on our guard against such attempts to pervert the course of justice,' I was told by one judge. An experienced Rota advocate absolutely refused to believe that a high degree of corruption existed. Only when he had been quietly corrected and advised by a younger colleague did he change his mind. Then, with bewildered regret in his voice, he said: 'I am told that you are right. Much as we regret it, there *is* corruption.'

There is: and it takes insidious, hard-to-detect forms. 'In most cases,' a lawyer explained, 'the client is only interested in one thing: ending his marriage. He knows he has no chance of doing so without things being "arranged" for him. In such cases we must first discover what the facts are; then we have to see if it is possible to set them in a certain light. In the majority of cases a client will maintain that he and his wife never really intended to make a lasting marriage. They will probably lack proof of this, but it is basically true. Our task, quite frankly, is to make the necessary evidence available.'

The means of providing this usually takes the form of a registered postcard. Ostensibly it was written and delivered through the mails *before* the marriage. A postcard, because the 'document' will thus be franked by the date stamp of the postal service. Evidence of this is firmly stamped and dated on the same piece of paper as the declaration. If the card appears to have been written by the prospective husband to his future wife, or vice versa, it will unquestionably provide material evidence of nullity, because a state of mind which makes vows of marriage without the intention of keeping them must invalidate the sacrament of marriage.

Yet even this vital exhibit may not be enough to uphold the petition. There will have to be witnesses who will swear, on oath, that they knew of the petitioner's state of mind before the marriage. 'Their testimony must be bought, of course,' said my lawyer informant, 'but with the enormous amount of public sympathy for Catholics held captive in these dead marriages, this is not the most difficult part of the arrangement.'

He smiled easily, a man untroubled by his conscience. But what of the cases where such grounds are not possible? And if children have been born during a marriage, this will surely disprove lack of intention to raise a family? Ah, yes, but not of failure to make a true matrimonial vow, I was assured. Then it is sometimes possible to 'arrange' a plea of impotence. 'Provided the client is prepared to pay for the necessary medical evidence, it can be a good cause,' my informant said.

The Rota will entertain petitions of this sort only where such impotence can be proved to have existed before the marriage, and to have continued since. The doctors require extraordinary knowledge of their client's intimate life to swear to that. 'The way it is done,' I was told, 'is to find a doctor who'll testify that the client was totally impotent *under certain conditions*, which are usually psychological. Should the doctor be challenged during the hearing by the Defender of the Bond, who has power to call independent medical experts and to demand separate examinations of the client, he can quite easily assert that the condition is not *always* in evidence.'

It may seem that duping the Rota is not too difficult; but we should not forget the skill and severity of this ancient court. My unscrupulous informants had a healthy respect for it. One told me: 'We do charge high fees, it is true. But the service we give has to be completely foolproof. Even *we* cannot be sure of its acceptance.'

Another said: 'The Rota can discount evidence because its tribunal may merely *feel* that a case for marriage nullity is not justified. It has enormous powers of discretion. And it does not have to be governed by the blackness or whiteness of the evidence, nor even by the sworn testimony of witnesses.'

Perhaps, therefore, it is sometimes justifiable for the lay lawyers to ask high payment for their services, though this cannot condone the methods used. But worse even than these are the blackmailers and other criminals attracted to the victims of these courts. I was told that a lucrative branch of the Italian underworld deals in little else.

These pariahs work on information of shady dealings. They ferret out situations resulting from the strictness of the courts and the corruption outside. Where a person in a respectable position has perjured himself, or evidence can be found of forgery committed on his behalf, it is not hard to extract payment for silence under threat of exposure.

By hearing of a couple who are pretending to be married while living together, the blackmailer can bring similar pressure to bear. A great many prominent Italians are paying regularly for such 'discretion'. Adultery is a crime as well as a sin in their country.

There was a whisper in Rome that a fruitless blackmail attempt had started the ordeal of a famous filmstar. When the blackmailer was rebuffed, so the story goes, he revenged himself by persuading an innocent Italian woman to denounce the couple. This woman, a religious zealot, was easily persuaded that it was her plain duty to take out civil charges against them for bigamy. She had, of course, no idea that she was being used as a tool of corruption.

That case is typical of many tragic situations thrown up by the stern code of the Catholic laws. The 'husband' had been married before. They had had two children before they decided to separate. When he fell in love with the beautiful actress who became his legal wife, he naturally wished for an annulment of his previous marriage. But he wished in vain. If it is true that he or his 'bride' refused the blackmailers' propositions, then they paid a high price. The secret of their alliance, once exposed, brought a terrible punishment in publicity and scandal.

An Italian lawyer with whom I discussed their situation in London said: 'How they suffered! But they should have known that in Italy one always has to pay a price for these things.' Such a cynical view is not uncommon; certainly not among the wealthier Italian sophisticates. Honest payment of income tax, and other state levies, is regarded there as the act of a simpleton. *Not* to pay bribes is equally unthinkable among people with enough money to do so.

After the war the situation existed where respectable citizens declared only half their estates for tax. They did so knowing they would be automatically assessed for twice as much, but on payment of a substantial bribe to an underpaid civil servant it was always possible to straighten out the difference. At the same time, of course, the bribes incidentally raised the civil servant's earnings to a living wage.

Upright Englishmen would find such methods unthinkable in their own country. But not a few have become embroiled in the corruption which surrounds the courts of the Church of Rome. It seems that this is a *modus vivendi* which must be accepted in the light of the general axiom: 'When in Rome, do as the Romans.' Some time ago, this built-in tolerance towards corruption caused wholesale profiteering by an ambitious Italian advocate. Until his death this man enjoyed a reputation for having discovered the 'Catholic Reno'.

There, unwanted marriages could be shed with an ease which appealed even to the laziest and the most puritanical; provided, that is, that they felt no qualms about the cost involved. The essence of the scheme depended on an accepted premise in Italian State law. By this, a marriage contracted legally outside the country may be ratified. Once such a marriage has received State approval by ratification, acceptance of any previous divorce is implicit, even though divorce remains illegal in Italy.

The lawyer who exploited this legal ambiguity built up a considerable fortune. An embittered ex-colleague explained to me: 'He took money in bucketfuls from hopeful petitioners. All he had to offer in return was a magical rabbit in his silk-hat; namely a close association with the Mexican town of Juarez.'

In Juarez, the divorce-and-remarriage mills of that tolerant country ground at their most productive. The town had machinery for dispensing both marriage and divorce, by double-proxy. Neither party needed to be present to receive blessing, sacrament, or anything more than the receipted bill. By adroit use of this mail-order form of contract-making-and-breaking, the Roman advocate led a considerable number of tragic husbands and wives out of one wedlock, and into another. Before he died suddenly, eight years ago, he had made over a score of visits to Juarez. On each occasion a pile of dossiers and portfolios, bulging with papers detailing his clients' cases, went with him.

This man is believed to have offered his services so widely that there are still married Catholics around the world who daily expect to hear news of their freedom. He was a man whose confidence and optimism spread rapidly to others. His blandest assurances that 'all will be well if you just leave matters in my hands' were taken at face value. He was liked and trusted. In fact, he had vastly more hope than certainty. The legal chicane he had discovered was soon noticed by the authorities, who waited only for an appropriately exemplary case before pouncing. But, while it lasted, the legal marriage-guide continued to trick hundreds out of their money.

His method was to insist on a heavy deposit. This, he said, was needed to defray heavy travelling and other costs. I have been assured that shortly before his death he combed more than a quarter of a million pounds out of a single French region in such advance fees. According to my informant, who claims to have irrefutable proof, the advocate knew when he accepted three hundred fees of a hundred pounds each from the people of St Julien, near Lac Leman in the Haute Savoie region of France, that he could not possibly secure their release from their marriages.

Escape, it seems, was only available in certain cases. The picturesque documents which the crooked advocate could provide were written in quaint Spanish. They were embossed with an impressive array of seals and ribbons. But they were worthless without official ratification by their own Commune. This the people of St Julien would have been powerless to obtain, had they ever needed to do so. Only the death of their self-appointed saviour prevented this discovery.

It did not, I believe, save a number of those who failed to negotiate the lawyer's documents in their own courts. He himself used an Italian part of Switzerland, in the Canton of Lugano, for the purpose of Italian ratification of marriages. Far fewer questions were asked in this remote spot. The authority vested in it gave all the necessary powers. But others were not so fortunate.

In Rome, I met one of the most prominent victims of the lawyers' marriage-mill. He was a rich, famous man, whose divorce had been obtained in Mexico; after which he had re-married in the same country. There had been no need, he told me, for either his wife or himself to be present at either ceremony. And the documents he received from his lawyer were said to be legally acceptable in Italy, and capable of ratification there. So, having paid the man's considerable fee, the husband was bitterly disappointed to discover that in fact none of the decrees and certificates he had bought were acceptable under Italian law. The bitter farce of this case was that both he and his new wife were in far worse a situation *as married people* than they would have been as illicit lovers; for in Italy the crime of bigamy carries a heavier penalty than that of adultery. Thus, as was quickly pointed out to them by their lawyer, the safest course was to dissolve their expensive Mexican 'marriage'; and this they did.

The most recent information I have, though neither is forthcoming about the legal complexities of their situation, points to a growing feeling among the State lawyers that this dissolution cannot indefinitely be any more acceptable than any other Italian divorce. It has not been ratified by a subsequent marriage, so that that loophole cannot be used as an escape-route. The unhappy couple, both unspeakably distressed after years of legal wrangling and threats of police action, are still liable to be dragged back almost to where they started, and for as long as they remain in Italy.

Whatever the outcome, is there no hope of either of them obtaining approval from the Church? The Rota has made it clear that it sees no cause for interference. The previous marriage remains good in their eyes. So the husband must stay in a state of spiritual bigamy with his second 'wife'.

The tragedy of these two may seem to merit more compassion than the Church is permitted to extend. They love each other, and they are not married to anyone else by any observable bond, except that of the spiritual vow, or sacrament, which one of them had once entered into. To add to the problem, there are children of the previous marriage. They are being brought up by a loving step-mother. But she cannot become their father's wife in other than name and the laws of a foreign country.

Whether or not these two lovers have sinned is a matter for their consciences; but, in a Church which possesses the supernatural powers of Christ's Church on earth, it may seem to the outsider that there is a curiously unbending attitude in regard to such sins. Furthermore, it is inescapable to the critical mind that all interpretations of the marriage vow are made in the Roman Catholic Church by celibates; for the most part, men who have had no experience whatever of normal love and its fulfilment. They are judging, in all these matters, from a coldly academic standpoint made no warmer, or more humane, by its assumption of being God's.

That tragic couple may, as my learned friend implied, have brought much of their problem on themselves, but their plight is not theirs alone. In Italy, there were recently close on one million couples living in adultery ('mortal sin') as a result of similar, irresolvable situations. Such spiritual outcasts may not avail themselves of confession, and so are cut off from the sacrament of the Holy Eucharist, their communion with Christ. They must live their spiritual lives in a shifty, conscience-smitten half-world, sentenced for as long as their Church holds to its absolute views.

It is no surprise therefore to learn that a cynical form of 'insurance' has become customary among many of the more sophisticated of these thwarted people. In this, a young girl about to be married will send her fiancé a pre-arranged postcard declaring in advance her determination not to have children, or her refusal to accept marriage for life. This document will be preserved (with what grim or jocular references!) during the early years of the marriage, in case it should happen to be required. If the couple decide to divorce, then the vital card will be produced as evidence to the courts. And it will be a most weighty evidence at that, since it is genuinely stamped and dated.

There will still be the necessity of producing witnesses to corroborate the statement, but properly organised 'insurances' or this sort rarely lack confederates. As I say, this is a game played mainly by the more sophisticated, but I am assured it is increasingly used, and was in the minds of the Italian senators who recently voted for their civil divorce Bill.

So we see that the tight-fast door, as always, produces a complex of corrupt avenues around it. These necessarily now involve many otherwise virtuous and devoted Catholics. In place of the 'Catholic Reno', which closed down with the death of its promoter, other escape routes have arisen, among them the tiny nation of San Marino. Here, the laws permit all necessary indulgence, provided the parties in a marriage have enjoyed residence in the principality for three years. So scores of those Italian couples, who can afford the legal and other costs involved, have become officially domiciled there for no other reason.

Prior to the Second World War the most acceptable escape-route lay through the cities of Budapest and Fiume. Catholics living in Italy could dissolve their marriage bonds in the Hungarian capital. Subsequently they could ratify a civil divorce in Fiume, on the borderline of Italy. But Russian occupation of the satellite countries, including Hungary, finally ended this loophole.

The tragedy is that the all-powerful and secret Sacred Rota court of Rome cannot prevent exploitation of these many illicit by-ways. By its insistence on what it believes to be the letter of God's 'natural law', no licence can be given. No Catholic may countenance any legal form of marriage dissolution, except on the terms we are already familiar with. The result is bound to be, for as long as this inflexible attitude remains, chicanery, legal manipulation, extortion of 'black' fees, and a corrosive destruction of moral standards among those most sorely tempted.

These are serious charges. The Roman Church does not like to hear them, or to be told the unpleasant facts supporting them. But it is well aware that they exist.

The Church, nevertheless, takes the view that it is entitled to believe in the honesty of its followers, and that this is a private concern and none of our business. Also, that if the courts are sometimes duped by perjury or ruse, then provided every proper care has been taken no blame can tarnish the spiritual reputation of the Church or the Rota. For this reason marriage cases are never allowed to be irrevocably decided. The courts' decisions, even when agreed at all *instances*, can *always* be reversed.

It is easy to appreciate this attitude when one realises that the Rota, and the lower courts, are mere instruments of Christ's laws as interpreted by the Catholic Church. Thus they can do no more than attempt solutions, they cannot provide them where they do not exist. Even so, the charges seem worthy of consideration when one takes into account the appalling and widespread suffering caused by such an unbending attitude.

It is not in doubt, I think, that thousands of Catholics are existing in anguish and bitterness; nor that faith and resolution fail in most cases to console such desperately frustrated human beings. We know that the Church has an answer to their plea for more human understanding, but can this always be justified? Are there no conditions abroad in the world today that would seem to any man or woman on earth, of whatever creed, to merit more the rule of the heart rather than the head? Can anyone hold that Christ would have denied freedom to some of the caged souls living today in unwanted marriage bonds?

These are questions etched out by this aspect of the Roman court, whatever its jurisprudent excellence and skill. They cry out for a sympathetic answer; but, alas, this is not in the power of the Church to give.

EIGHT

Stony Ground

In May 1964 the secretary of the tribunal of a large American diocese sat at his typewriter to complete a brief, business-like letter to a man in Florida. Probably, he gave it little more thought than the rest of his correspondence. But this single, typed sheet was to impose an extraordinarily harsh ban on the man to whom it was addressed. One that explains much about the ways of the marriage courts of the Catholic Church towards those outside it.

The note was inoffensive. It said, merely: 'Dear Mr A, We regret to inform you that all efforts, including those of the Archdiocese, to obtain the testimonies of your former wife, and of her husband, have failed. . . . Assuring you a remembrance in our prayers, I remain, Sincerely yours in Christ.' Et cetera.

The effect was to shut out from the Catholic Church a man who had hoped to become a member of that faith, and who wanted, above everything, to marry his second wife within it. Why was it necessary to forbid his entry? From facts examined already, it may be thought that Catholics are often more harshly treated by their courts than outsiders, indeed canon law can seem far less tolerant towards the faithful than to others. The truth is demonstrated by this case.

Some of the most poignant victims of the Church's law are Christian non-Catholics, those who seek to enter the

Roman faith in order to marry one who holds it. Mr A and his first wife had been divorced, and now he wanted to marry a Catholic. The snag was that, in Rome's eyes, the first Mrs A had been married before, and any subsequent union was out of the question.

The American tribunal secretary was therefore instructed to act only on this basic reasoning, which set in high relief the problems of those who live by one set of rules and try to join their life to another. Mr A's case failed because of lack of co-operation by his former wife and her former husband. Hundreds of Christian cases are equally unacceptable to the Church of Rome. And many are prevented from becoming Catholics by these strict rules.

But is there nothing the Church can do to help them? It appears not. Unless the would-be convert and his would-be bride or groom is prepared to lead a 'brother and sister' relationship, the union cannot be blessed by the Church. In this case the second Mrs A was already a Catholic. She had not known of her husband's earlier wife's *previous* marriage until shortly before their wedding. He had not thought it important enough to mention to her, but when she learned the facts she did everything in her power to get an annulment of her future husband's earlier marriage. The grounds were that his first wife, being already married, had not been free to marry him, and this was the plea which failed.

The future Mrs A, though the daughter of an Episcopalian, was a devoted member of her Church. She had always assumed her fiancé would have married her in her Church if he had not been prevented, by his earlier marriage, from doing so. When he mentioned casually that his first wife had been married before, she recognised that in the law of her Church (*indeed, in her own belief*) he was free to marry her.

As his previous marriage had never existed, the sacrament would bless their union. Only one obstacle lay in the way of this: it had to be proved that the previous Mrs A's *first husband* had been alive when she and Mr A were married. With only forty eight hours to spare, the problems facing the future Mrs A were acute.

What should she do? Her fiancé was so obviously blameless; indeed, he had no idea of what this knowledge could mean to her. He wanted them to marry, and the civil ceremony was all arranged, for as he explained he had never doubted that his earlier marriage was genuine. In his own Church's view, and that of the law of the land, it was. How could he have guessed that it might be the key to his entry into the Roman Church?

The future Mrs A begged him to promise that, if she married him now in the civil ceremony, he would later do all he could to establish the nullity of his first marriage, and then re-marry her in her own Church.

Of course, Mr A did so with complete confidence and joy. He felt strongly that his wife and he should share a mutual faith. But, after they had been wed, with only the flutter of Mrs A's conscience to disturb the serenity of the occasion, an unexpected difficulty arose. The first Mrs A's earlier husband, and the first Mrs A, refused to help the suit.

The newly-married couple went to her priest for immediate advice. He cautioned Mr A against becoming a Catholic until after the annulment: 'Otherwise, your earlier marriage will have to be accepted, and your present union will be held adulterous in the Church,' he warned. The couple then set to work.

Mrs A has since explained: 'I went to a great deal of trouble. It meant getting all the papers together, birth certificates, baptismal certificates, First Holy Communion, Confirmation, signed and witnessed by a priest. It was quite a job.' Statements from her parents had to attest that she had been brought up a Catholic. Then there was the business of getting copies of her husband's first wife's *first* marriage and divorce papers, and also legal proof of his marriage and divorce. 'We thought everything was fine,' Mrs A said sadly. 'When, at last, we had assembled everything, it seemed there couldn't be anything else needed.'

And the priest did accept the documents willingly, passing them on, in Mr A's name, to the local Diocesan Tribunal. It was only then that the first setback arose to disturb the hopeful couple. 'We will require further proof of these,' they were told, 'in the form of testimonies by Mr A's former wife and her previous husband. Will you please put us in touch with them?'

Mr A was bewildered. He knew that his first wife was unlikely to help, as there was a deep and bitter gulf between them, yet every possible attempt had to be made. The present Mrs A recalls these moments with great distress. 'It was awful,' she said. 'She had been crazy about my husband, for a long while before they married, apparently, but he wouldn't marry her. That is why she married her first husband, out of pure spite! After a year and a half, she came to my husband and asked him to help her to get a divorce, saying her marriage was "impossible".'

The second Mrs A's contempt for such manœuvres was plain: 'She really got to work,' she said. 'Dyed her hair blonde, took up smoking and drinking. She even gave up being a vegetarian. Finally, she threw herself at my husband, got herself pregnant, so that he had to make an "honest woman" of her. She then had an abortion because she didn't want an "early" baby. Need I say more?'

Now that the first wife refused help, Mr and Mrs A's disappointment could be imagined. In Mrs A's words: 'We were right back where we started. Even to get to this point had taken an entire year. We had been married in April 1963, and the letter from the tribunal was dated 12th May 1964.' She showed me the letter.

In it the tribunal secretary explained why he could not go on with their case. He said: 'The reason for the failure is the fact that [your previous wife] absolutely refused to testify and has persuaded [her previous husband] to do the same. Unless we can obtain the co-operation of the above-named persons it will be impossible for us to process your case and we will necessarily have to abandon it.'

So ended an attempt by a good Catholic to marry, out of love, a man she sincerely believed has never been married before, *either by her Church's law or her own conviction*. He had been married under the law of her land, but that was not the point at issue.

She, too, is legally married now, but this does not make her feel properly joined to her husband. What she seeks is full, spiritual and sacramental union with this man, to complete—in her terms—'the cycle of their love'. She may not have it, because one jealous woman had the power to stand against the whole force of canon law. As Mrs A says: 'Now, all we can do is pray that my husband's "ex" will change her mind.'

It is sad that the most powerful Church in the world has no authority over such changes of heart, but absolute proof is demanded by its courts in every case, however harrowing. The reason for forcing this couple to live spiritually apart is that they failed to bring proof of nullity of the previous marriage. It is pointless to ask why such extraordinary dogmatism should be applied when the rule of a tolerant God is supposedly under consideration.

The following account concerns another tragic victim of the courts, a woman well-known in Paris society, Madame Maud. She feels no bitterness towards the Roman Church, accepting its edict with humble regard for its known and great virtues, but she has suffered deeply.

'This is my second marriage,' she told me. 'For that reason I cannot become a Roman Catholic as my heart and

87

my head both urge me to do. In every way I want this, but it is impossible, both for me and for my husband.'

Madame Maud explained how her husband had agreed to enter the Catholic Church with her, to have children and to bring them up in the Church. She said: 'We both thought this would give them the healthiest and finest upbringing possible. Together, we approached canon lawyers in Paris for their advice. We were told that there was nothing to prevent our joining the Church, indeed the priest we talked to said it would be welcomed. He said we must first take instruction in the faith, and suggested we went to the Benedictines. But it was there that a nasty shock was waiting for us.

'My husband and I were told we had two choices: either we could sacrifice our marriage and become Catholics, or we could stay as we were—heretics in the eyes of the Church—and remain married. The reason naturally was that I had been married before, or, as they put it, "remained married". Hence my marriage to my husband, once we became Catholics, would cease to exist.'

As a result of this advice, Madame Maud's feelings towards her Church changed. Yet after a time she began to feel a desire to struggle against such 'absolute expulsion', and looked for legal grounds on which to do so. Again she consulted learned Catholic priests; but this time she asked many questions she had not asked before. About the nature of marriage and divorce within the Catholic faith. Slowly, the dawning of fresh hope began.

Annulment had previously been explained to her, but she now learnt something of the intricate and complex reasons for these 'dead' bonds. Among other points was the well-known and frequent cause of 'lack of intention' to have children. When such a condition could be proved to have been part of a union, she was told, it would certainly not have been a marriage.

Madame Maud, at this point, bitterly remembered her previous husband's open and determined refusal to have a family. When she mentioned this to her priest friends, they were optimistic. It was pointed out that the following year was to be a 'Year of Grace' in Rome, which occurs only once every twenty five years. During these, any petitioner may take a matrimonial case appeal direct to the Rota in Rome.

For a while it seemed that fortune would favour Madame Maud's case, but then snags began to appear. As a Protestant, she was told, she could not seek papal indulgence (whether or not this advice was accurate, it was given to her). She was also told that, if she became a Catholic, it would endanger her marriage. Indeed, the timing was not in her favour at all.

As a priest put it to her: 'You are not still in your twenties! I know you want to marry and have children above everything else, but if you appeal to Rome now and become an RC then, before your case has cleared the first two hurdles of *first* and *second instances*, the Grace Year will have come and gone. Look at these . . .'

He opened a cupboard to show her shelves filled with green file boxes. Each contained a matrimonial suit waiting for the Rota's attention. Her petition would have to join onto the tail-end of this queue—and it represented only a fraction of the work piling up in similar diocesan offices around the world. 'It may take you three years, or longer, to get what you want,' he warned. 'Which means that you will have to postpone your marriage at least for that time.'

He looked at her, she says, with kindly understanding. 'I don't even ask what you are going to do,' he murmured. 'I know, and you will be forgiven.' In a quiet, gentle voice, she says he advised her: 'Be wise. Marry now, as a non-Catholic, and bring up your children as Roman Catholics.

My child, do not waste what remains of your youth. I will give you my benediction.'

Madame Maud later explained: 'I did as he suggested, and today my two daughters, aged thirteen and eleven, are Roman Catholics. But neither I nor my husband can go to Church with them.' On the day the girls took their first Communion, their mother was offered the sacrament. The officiating priest, who knew her story, had sympathised. But his kindly action only enlarged the bitter irony of her situation.

It happened that this priest was unusually tolerant—even daring—in doing what he did. Yet Madame Maud felt she could not take advantage of his generosity. 'I simply couldn't bring myself to take Communion with my daughters,' she said. 'I knew I had no right to this sacrament of their Church.' Finally, she arranged for someone else to accompany them. As she says: 'I thought it was the best thing to do for their sake.'

She paused, deeply moved by the memory of an occasion when she had had to refuse to share the worship and spiritual fulfilment of her children. Then she said slowly: 'For myself, there can be no entry into the Church, yet it is the one I admire above all others. As long as I stay married to my husband this has to be. Of course it hurts . . .'

Passionately, she added: 'Don't you think it is painful for a mother to have no answers to questions from her own daughters? When they were home on holiday from their convent school they wanted to know why we had no photograph of our wedding. All their friends had pictures of *their* mothers in white bridal veils, standing at the Church door with the priests beside them. I forget what I told them, but soon afterwards they went back to school and later I heard how they had explained this to one of the Sisters who taught them. '*Our mother was never properly married*, they said.'

The bitterness with which this mother uttered these words should have been heard in the cool, slow-moving offices of the Sacred Rota. Her's is not a particularly unusual case. Thousands of similarly thwarted parents are living spiritually apart from their own children. The choice offered by the Catholic Church is fair and just according to its law, but is the law itself fair?

Madame Maud's stumbling-block was the slow, traditional machinery of matrimonial canon law. Yet this is how it is applied throughout the vast Roman Catholic world. According to this, she could never have been married in the eyes of God since her first husband refused to give her children, therefore no quick, speedy action could free her.

She and her family must live their lives deprived of something they deeply and seriously want. It is for the Church of Rome, now so active in other works of internal revolution, to decide whether these tragic cases are not urgent reminders of a great need for change. In a community so large, victims of circumstances will always be found. But it would be strange if this consideration should ever be used as an implacable shield against tolerance.

From the United States a man wrote to tell of his Roman Catholic aunt's burial. As a girl, she had gone to America from England. Before becoming a Roman Catholic, she had had three husbands. Yet all these marriages were declared null by Rome and she was allowed to marry a fourth time, in the Church. This fourth, or real, husband meant a great deal to her, more than any of the others had done. His death, in a hit-and-run accident which she witnessed, came as a terrible blow.

According to doctors, the shock was so great that her mind was permanently injured. It was this, so her nephew says, which caused her to take both to 'drink and admirers'. When she died in Detroit the poor woman was refused burial in a Catholic cemetery. Her fourth husband lay buried there, and she had reserved her grave beside him. But the priest refused to bury her. The reason given was that at the time of her death she had been 'living in sin': a bitter, indeed, stunning, blow to her non-Catholic family, but especially so in the circumstances.

Her nephew recalls. 'At about the same time, one of the wealthy Patino family had died of an overdose of sleeping pills. Yet she was taken into St Patrick's Cathedral in New York for a grand funeral!' The question he asks is: 'If one Catholic cannot be accepted by the Church, how can another equally dubious case be given its fullest honours?' But such questions are seldom answered. Inside the Church of Rome silence is held to be the best policy when such disputes arise. The results, regrettably, are measurable in human suffering.

Another American case occurred in 1963. From it one can see how those on the perimeter of a Catholic marriage problem can become involved. In Pittsburg, California, a young man married a Roman Catholic girl. The wedding was in the girl's church and she had been told, so the bridegroom's mother later claimed, that 'during the ceremony a miracle would take place, and she would love him'. No such miracle, unfortunately, occurred and the bride found herself married to a man she did not and could not love, but who was now her husband for eternity.

His distressed mother told me: 'Unloved, my son developed a personality certainly far different from his former, dear self.' This led him to behave harshly towards his wife, and finally there was a civil divorce. But in the wife's eyes she was still married. Even when he had married again, and given his second wife three children, she persisted in this belief.

The mother now questions the humaneness of this faith. 'What good can there be,' she asks, 'in a Church which chains a good and sensitive young woman to a marriage that never grew to be one?' Her son, she says, now declares openly that he is 'glad [he] is not a Christian'. His reason is that Christians appear to be 'traditionally unmerciful and horribly cruel'. His mother says further: 'This poor Roman Catholic girl had no money to pay for an annulment by the Sacred Rota. She could only pray for my son's death to free her to marry again.' And she asks: 'Telling a young girl to expect a miracle can only be a delusion—not *faith*—surely? Are they not guilty of breach of faith?'

Whoever advised the girl to expect a miraculous change of heart may well be; but perhaps it is too late to consider righting whatever wrongs lie in this tangled skein. Some few weeks after our correspondence on this matter had lapsed I heard again from the distressed mother. This time she wrote: 'Since writing to you, my former daughter-in-law (the dear, innocent little Roman Catholic who really believed that some miracle would take place when she was married to my young teenage son in her Church) suddenly remarried without consulting her priest. Nor did she inform her mother, or any of the "good" people responsible for her terrible heartaches, mental anguish and nervous collapse. In my opinion this nervous breakdown was a direct result of unimaginable pressures—a sort of combination of the Oriental plot and the Spanish Inquisition. My son, as I well know, suffered from it too.' She concluded: 'No wonder poor Jesus still hangs there bleeding and dying for all the sins of the world!'

It is hard to comment without fuller examination of this case, but an obvious criticism must be made of anyone who, in the name of Religion, offers inducements to marriage based on powers which it does not possess. If a priest told the girl to expect a miracle, then he was acting not only improperly—the Holy Office would condemn such mystic meddling—but inhumanly as well. As the result achieved is finally of no gain to the Church, it is perhaps of little consequence. But the scar left on the heart of this mother, and on her son who was cruelly deceived, will not lightly be forgotten.

NINE

Rebels

The film *Divorce, Italian Style* portrays a Sicilian baron behaving like a homicidal Walter Mitty. In his dreams of getting rid of his Catholic wife to marry a girl he passionately desires, he eventually conceives an idea of killing the wife without fatal risk, by making her murder appear as a *crime passionel*. This involves introducing the wife's old lover, leaving them together, writing himself anonymous letters detailing an intrigue between them, then killing them both.

As intended, the baron is arrested and charged. But sympathy in his village reduces his sentence to only three years' imprisonment. Then he is freed to marry the girl for whom he murdered his wife. The ceremony—and this was the irony of the film—takes place in church, amid general rejoicing, with the bride in virginal white. Priests solemnly bless the couple.

Strangely, it passed unnoticed that this cynical film was allowed to be shown in Italy *without cuts*. Italian censorship is among the strictest in the world. There is no right of appeal for those who suffer from it. No abuse of its elaborate code of laws—largely inspired by the Church—is tolerated, yet this obvious satire went unmolested.

The reason, I was told in Rome, was that the film had been deliberately made to expose all the worst aspects of Catholic Italian marriage, but made in such a way that it would not attract the censor's blue-pencil. Brilliantly, the work had succeeded in doing just that. It delighted a small group of talented and highly critical cinema artists, led by the film's director, Pietro Germi, but it escaped censure.

Latent rebels against the bonds of the Church are not hard to find in Italy. Their numbers increase the nearer they are to Rome, but the wide popularity of this daring spoof has been an indication of more than artistic rebellion.

How much real justification have these revolutionaries? At a time when Catholics are involved in increasing criticism, both in and out of their Church, they may claim more than is usual. But the Roman Church is used to criticism, and to change. It has the immutable, subtle power of institutions which outlast the centuries. It can contain almost any attack, even though the new and surprisingly total legalisation of civil divorce in the Italian courts may prove a major set-back to its temporal powers.

This is not to say that the Church makes no attempt to move with the times. In July 1964, it allowed a Catholic American, Patrick C. Barker, to marry an Episcopalian girl, Susan Ekberg, in a 'mixed' ceremony, which took place in a Roman Catholic Church, in St Louis with a 'heretical' Episcopalian minister officiating jointly with a Catholic priest. Since Catholic canon law insists on children of mixed marriages being brought up as Catholics, the marriage was unique. Yet it had the full approval of both Churches' leading representatives on the spot.

Other pointers to Rome's new and broader-minded attitudes can be seen in the wedding ceremony itself. Where previously the ceremonial was read *before* the nuptial Mass, it has now been raised to the important position following the gospel. There are significant hints, too, in many recent public statements of Catholic theologians showing a liberality and tolerance towards divorce which would have been unthinkable only five years ago. These and other liberal cries are growing stronger all the time. In the USA especially, scholars, theologians and others are openly questioning the Church's assumptions of divine law. Such progressives assert with passion that the marriage rules are governed by ecclesiastical edicts only. They point to the Church's doctrine, that the sacrament is conferred by the couple, not by the priest, who is a mere witness.

Boldness of this kind might have been punished by death in the time of the Spanish inquisition. Today it is part of a sincere and thrusting curiosity taking root in the universal Catholic mind. Can we say that the rebels are backed by locical, even irrefutable, facts? Cases before the Rota would appear to do little or nothing to disprove this.

Two years ago in Geneva a tormented Englishman was fighting to free himself from a civilly-dissolved marriage. He wanted to marry a Catholic girl whom he deeply loved. But the Church will allow no 'outsider' baptised in the Christian faith to marry if he has previously contracted marriage. So this young man, who is a member of the Church of England as was his first wife, is still married in Rome's eyes. He is placed no differently in this situation from cases we have already examined, but there are interesting complications.

He is now living in what the Church defines as 'mortal infamy and sin'. The girl he wants to wed shares his home, they have been married civilly, and he has fathered her child. Whether they will ultimately be allowed to marry in the Church will depend on the matrimonial tribunal. But his plea is straightforward: that his first wife refused to have children.

Could he not wait? His difficulties arose from the length of time taken by the courts. He told me: 'My case has taken two years. From time to time I find myself infuriated over the delay and frustration of it all. But what can I do? It seems it is not done to complain. But how can it be justice to smother proceedings in such an aura of mystery? What's worse is that I feel sure that this is intentional, to make people give up.'

He went on: 'I am not a Catholic, but I am being greatly helped by a canon lawyer of the Church of Rome. There I have no complaint. But he is my advocate, and the case seems to me to be plain-sailing, really, so why doesn't he get on with it? He tells me he's having a hard job tracking down all my witnesses. I suppose this is understandable. But so far the case has not even cleared *first instance*! Goodness knows how much longer it will take.' He shook his head anxiously, and added: 'Or what it will cost.'

Later, he explained: 'One of the things one is battling against the whole time is an extraordinary degree of vagueness. Clerks in the courts are not always clear whether documents should be written in Latin or not. Nobody seems to know whether my case will be dealt with at *second instance* in a regional appeal court or whether it will have to go straight up to Rome. Why? Why is there all this confusion? My first wife is in sympathy with the suit, so there is no formidable problem that I can see. As to costs, well, I am just sitting here and hoping it will not be too expensive. Meanwhile there is *nothing* that I can do. Believe me, it is not a very pleasant situation.'

Assisting this petitioner was an official of an English diocese, a young Catholic lawyer-priest, well-trained in the intricacies of canon law. And he too had criticisms. 'Ignorance is the main trouble,' he told me. 'It is marked, even among priests. For instance, almost no Catholic in England knows whether he may have to take his case to the Rota in Rome, and often he has no idea what is in store when he starts the suit; no idea at all!'

The same expert made a strong plea for reform. The appeal insisted on by Rome in all marriage cases seemed to him a waste of time. 'We Catholics grumble about civil courts,' he said, 'accusing them of tolerating corruption and other weaknesses. And we refuse to accept their evidence and go to great lengths to obtain our own. But are we so much better? Why should our cases have to go to appeal as a matter of form? If the delay involved in this could be cut out, our justice would be far more humane.'

A rebel? In Rome I asked a judge of the Rota what he thought of this priest's suggestion. He said it was 'not politic' for a junior lawyer (though an official of the matrimonial courts) to offer such basic criticisms. He told me severely: 'The lower courts are always blaming the Rota for delays, but the fault lies with them. If they were more efficient, we should have less work to do on appeal here in Rome.'

Many priests and lawyers, nevertheless, share the rebellious official's view. Reform, they say, is urgently needed. They refuse to accept Rome's view that delays stem mainly from the lower courts. One claimed proudly: 'In our diocese, we have *never* had a nullity case lasting more than six months.'

This official's reputation among Catholics in his parish was high. They recognised him as a lawyer who practised with humanity is well as respect and knowledge of the law. In a seven-year period, between January 1956 and December 1963, his diocesan tribunal had dealt with fifty-nine cases. Fifty-three of these had received affirmative decisions. In Rome, successful cases seldom rise above half those heard, though it must be said that of these most have received conflicting verdicts in the lower courts.

An English marriage court official told me that his most difficult duty lay in instructing non-Catholics about to marry Catholics. He had to try to show them the whole inner meaning and nature of the bond they are to share. As he said: 'It is often far from easy. People come here with stardust in their eyes. When in love nothing else matters to them. They probably do not take in more than one word in ten I say.'

A problem here is that non-Catholics marrying in the Roman Church are just as bound to understand the meaning of the vows as are Catholics. Their intention in regard to the marriage must conform with the code of canon law. So a prenuptial enquiry is put to them. It asks, among other searching questions: 'Do you understand the chief ends, the rights and obligations of marriage?' Also: 'Do you both intend to contract marriage in accordance with the teachings of the Catholic Church?' and, 'Do you both intend to contract marriage without and reservations or conditions to your consent?'

The person who signs his, or her, name to that is afterwards bound to be treated, in canon law, as though fully entered into the sacrament of holy matrimony, as interpreted by Rome. Yet these conditions may seem unimportant to the non-Catholic. The late Michael Canfield, who once believed himself married to Princess Lee Radziwill, was able to explain this from personal experience. 'I was never accepted into the Church,' he told me. 'All we got was a dispensation from somebody. Then I had to take what I facetiously describe as "six easy lessons", from a priest.' Canfield was in New York at the time. He explained that there was a worldly Jesuit who 'dined a lot' with his future bride and him. 'He seemed quite happy with the arrangement,' Canfield remembered. 'I suppose it was only a form of lip-service, but it satisfied the requirements.'

Later, Mr Canfield learnt that it was far from being 'only a form of lip-service'. His marriage was declared null as a result of things which he says he was never told about. It seems that Canfield's signing of the pre-nuptial enquiry form had left him no appeal. Thus, he was forced to accept the decisions of the Church absolutely. Had he wanted to keep his wife, only civil law could have helped him, but civil law has no power over the law of the Church in its own domain.

Critics point to these apparent anomalies, asking why the prelates of Rome appear to make no reforms to reduce secrecy and increase efficiency in the marriage courts. But in Rome one prominent British businessman who had recently been involved with the marriage courts seemed more baffled than angered when I interviewed him. He told me: 'Before I married, I always believed it was a matter of how much you paid. Now I know that it is much more a question of how well you have faked your evidence.'

This man went on to explain: 'Our situation arose because I, a reasonably good Roman Catholic, married a girl who was a Catholic only on paper. I met her when she was seventeen. We were married two years later. All went well until her mother came to live in the flat above us. A spiritual gap began to develop between my wife and myself. Whatever we did to try to bridge it only seemed to make it wider and finally my mother-in-law, who had been taking an increasing interest in our problems, suggested a short separation.

'Well, I thought it was to be only temporary. But, in fact, she persuaded my wife to go to the Regional Diocesan Court and start annulment proceedings. When I heard, I was literally flabbergasted. Twice, I had to attend hearings. I was told my wife's grounds—something about her not having "fully understood that the sacrament was lasting". I was astonished, and said so. But how could anyone deny it?

'Anyway, her first petition was thrown out, but the appeal was heard at the same court, and fresh evidence was brought, this time by her lawyer. Don't ask me what kind of evidence. I was not told. I *think* they had some letters testifying to her lack of understanding of the bond. And the *second instance* hearing was approved, she won an affirmative decision. I say "she", but it was really her mother's victory, because she was behind it all.'

He continued: 'Now, the big question was whether the Rota would approve or deny the suit. I was asked whether I would like to add anything, or merely confirm what I had previously said. As I really knew nothing of my wife's state of mind at the time referred to in the evidence, I could hardly say more. So a decision was given without me.

'I was surprised to learn from it *that I had never been married!* My two children had been born only in what is called in the Church "putative" or supposed wedlock. As to their future custody, the Rota made no suggestions of any kind. They appeared not to be interested in these children, who now have no true father or mother. We were left to work their fate out ourselves. We have never gone to law over them, because we both feel that they have suffered quite enough already. As for ourselves . . . well, what can I say? All the questions have been answered.'

Except one: what became of this man's marriage? As he said, 'I thought I was married with a family. Then suddenly, I'm told it never happened.' Thoughtfully, he added: 'As to my wife's "ignorance" . . . it *could be* that she did not know. It *could be* . . .' And gazing sorrowfully, if somewhat doubtfully, out of his office window over the rooftops of Rome, he smiled. I gained a strong impression that only this man's faith stood between him and a cry of revolt against the powers that have swept his home, and family, aside like so many crumbs.

Would it be unfair to let this single case blur the overall picture of the Catholic marriage courts? Yes, but such human considerations seem too often treated with clinical detachment by the skilled jurists of the Rota. The diocesan courts are little better. We cannot have it both ways, it will be argued. In pressing for more tolerance from the Church of Rome towards those locked in unwanted marriages, we cannot ask in the same breath for the protection of husbands from their wives' annulment suits. But the question raised is not quite this.

It involves the strength and morality of a law which will say that a marriage never happened *in God's eyes*; a law interpreted by man—and celibate man at that—which refuses to accept the contrasting evidence of the parties' experiences. This husband was unable to deny his wife's claim that she had never accepted the sacrament of holy marriage as binding for life. His own opinions were never fully considered, or they would have shown that, in his view, his family life was a vital reality. His wife's 'false intention', if it truly existed, could not have denied the fact of this. Her alleged 'condition' had not prevented her marrying, or having his children. Yet she was freed on her own word, supported by her mother's evidence. In the presentation of evidence the man she no longer chose to regard as her husband was strangely at her mercy.

Another case increasingly demonstrates the odd form taken by some of the difficulties thrown up by the Roman marriage courts. The rebels feel that their cause is strongly supported by such cases, but the facts were supplied by a judge of the Sacred Rota itself. During the Second World War a young Scots soldier met a girl in Glasgow, she a Roman Catholic like himself. Before he was sent overseas to a battle zone, they were married, but when the soldier came home, some two years later, he found that 'the lass had gone awa' ', as they say in that part of the world.

Very properly, the deserted husband took his distress to his priest, asking what could be done. Nothing could be done. The marriage sacrament, explained the priest, takes no account of desertion. It does not diminish by reason of the failure of a marriage *as* a marriage.

It is, the heartbroken soldier was told, eternal, constant, and irrevocable. In his Church's eyes, the husband would be a married man to the end of his days. Having no wife made no difference. He was married before God, and married he must remain. So he was not free to marry again, and never would be.

To non-Catholics this may seem monstrous, but in the Roman faith it is an unshakeable tenet of life. The Church cannot change quickly, if at all, to suit circumstances. When the husband pleaded with his priest, he was reminded of his comparative good fortune. 'Think,' he was told. 'If you had been walking down Sauchiehall Street last night, and a drunken driver had run into you, injuring your legs, how much worse off might you have been! You might have had both legs amputated, or worse. Could you honestly blame God for the accident, and ask Him to reverse His decision? Of course not. So why ask the Lord now for special treatment in the case of your marriage? You must live with it, my son, knowing that you are the helpless, but innocent, victim of a tragic accident.'

Whether or not the serviceman did live with it (is still doing so, perhaps?) the judge could not say. But the rebels would insist that, either way, it was no solution to the problem. The soldier could have obtained a civil divorce from his wife easily enough, but to do so he would have needed permission from his bishop. And this would only have been granted with the most extreme reluctance.

Without it, he would no longer have been able to go to confession. Admission of his sin would have brought an order to undo it and make penance, so he was trapped. Yet what was his sin? The Church claims allegiance to the 'natural laws'. What is more natural than a man's wish to sever a dead limb, or to grow a fresh branch where one has been lopped from his life? This wretched man would have had to go outside the Church he loved, but only because

the Church was powerless to help him. By its strict interpretation of the law of God such victims of cruel circumstances
can expect no mitigation.

It is only when rebellious minds weigh this principle
against the extraordinary power vested in the controversial
and comparatively recent 'infallibility' of the Pope, that it
becomes questionable. To acknowledge vicarious divine
power in a human being, with authority to dissolve *certain*
marriages, is one thing: a pope is a pope. But to hold
out empty hands to others in equal need seems curiously
inconsistent.

The laws of the Church are now being re-codified. A
changing attitude towards the marriage bonds may one day
take into account the nature of these criticisms. If and when
that happens, I believe many Catholics will feel easier in
their hearts.

This lip-service to dogma among Catholics often seems
faintly ludicrous to those outside the Church. In Rome, a
Catholic woman told me a story of a girl who married a
man she loved, after her parents had forbidden the match.
She went outside the Church to marry him. As with so
many of these headstrong affairs, the marriage did not last.

The young couple were civilly divorced, and then the girl
met a Roman Catholic and fell deeply in love again. She
could not marry him in his Church, and he would not
marry her outside it.

Fortunately there were strong grounds for nullity, but
this also happened during the war, and nobody could say
how long Rome would take to settle the case. In London,
where the ex-wife lived, an official listened to her story and
advised her to marry in a Register Office and forget the
Church courts, at least for the time being. The man she
loved was a pilot, and pilots' lives were not good risks.
'Once you are married,' the priest told her, 'come to us and
say that you felt you could not wait. Your fiancé was in

danger of being killed at any minute. In that case, I believe Rome will hurry matters along for you.'

Strange advice, one might think, even in war-time. But it was followed with complete success. Told of the circumstances, and of how the Catholic girl had already re-married civilly, Rome granted a nullity of the first marriage without any of its usual delay. A hidden pulse of human warmth? Canon lawyers tell me that it was more probably a wish to abate a possible scandal. Anyway, it was pointless, for the pilot was killed when he was about to fly home on leave. His bride had arranged to meet him in a London hotel, and they had planned to marry again, in the Church. When he did not arrive, she refused to leave.

Even when the news of his death was broken to her, she utterly rejected it. Finally, a friend had to force her into a car and take her home. Six months later the Church made one of its oddly sentimental gestures. The demented widow was allowed to go through a nuptial Mass *alone*. So that her parents should feel she was truly married, in the eyes of God, the marriage service was conducted as though the dead man was there. If the meaning was obscure (as there could be no sacrament possible with the dead) the ritual was believed, by the Church, to be of some slight comfort.

Before such a display of generosity let non-Catholics hold their counsel. Yet in one important particular the instance is worth considering. It shows that Rome *can* unbend its inflexible code of laws; the Church *is* capable of profound goodness of heart. Why, we may feel like asking, does it not show this quality more often? So many of its faithful followers live in spiritual torment. Is the plight of these souls, many of them outcasts from the Church they love, any less than the plight of the girl whose story has just been recounted?

TEN

Why Children Matter

One major virtue of Catholic upbringing is an obedience to faith which rarely questions too disturbingly, or at too much depth. Over the years this discipline has made it possible for the marriage courts to reach, unopposed, some of their strangest and most arguable decisions. And nowhere, I think, is this more noticeable to the outsider than in cases where the plea of nullity has been based on faulty intention.

Faulty intention simply means that one or the other, or both, of the marriage partners entered the marriage falsely. That they had held secret reservations, or that they had decided in advance that the vows they were making would be offered without any real intention of carrying them out.

Where this has occurred the marriage in Catholic eyes is not, and never was, a marriage. It has merely the outward semblance, a meaningless ceremony without the unifying, mystic grace of the sacrament to bind it. It is therefore highly eligible for a decree of annulment by the courts.

The difference which marks out this form of nullity from others is that it involves children. Where it can be proved that there was a declared intention not to have children by the marriage, nullity is assured. Though there are other basic faults of intention (private refusal to accept the marriage as eternal, and ceremonies deliberately perverted, as by the exclusion of a proper witness, are two of them) this lack of willingness to procreate is most frequently brought to the courts.

It is interesting to note other countries' laws in this regard. In Britain, marriage is described as 'the union of a man and woman for life'. There is nothing on the statute book to define its legal purpose. Whether or not the parties wish to have children is left to them. There have been civil actions about this which have produced a number of verdicts on both sides.

In the USA, the situation is reversed. There the marriage bond seems to be held in almost Catholic respect as regards its offspring. 'With the object of constituting a family' is a phrase often heard in civil definitions. As F. J. Sheed has pointed out: 'A Catholic canonist could hardly put it more strongly.'

But, if Protestants vary, there has never been the slightest doubt in Catholic opinion on the essential issue of true marriage. It is therefore all the more surprising that so many nullity pleas are registered on this score.

Lack of intention to have children is one of the most common of all causes pleaded, and it is abundantly clear that a great many of the suits brought every year in its name do genuinely represent true experiences and histories of the petitioners. On the other hand there are scandalous exceptions. In 1922, a wealthy man fell madly in love with a prostitute. When he insisted on marrying her his friends persuaded him to make one condition in advance. It was this: *He would absolutely and completely reject any suggestion of children being born of the marriage.*

In due course the man's passion cooled, but he had taken his friends' advice, and so a case for nullity was presented on his behalf to the marriage courts. On appeal, it came before the Rota. The grounds? Naturally that the man had obstructed the sacrament by excluding procreation from his vows.

A respected brother and an independent lawyer were among the friends who vouched for this evidence. The court held their testimony sufficient, and nullity was granted. A rich man's gratitude no doubt compensated his helpers, but how morally right had their friendly action been?

Ethically, the courts do not concern themselves with the degree of sin revealed during the hearing of a marriage case. The conduct of petitioners and witnesses is left to the individuals' consciences. But sharp rebukes, often in quaint Latin, are occasionally handed down by the judges. Petitioners can be strongly rebuked, and Excommunication may even result, from disclosures during a case.

Was the rich man such a sinner? In non-Catholic eyes it might be argued that he had only taken reasonable precaution against the collapse of his marriage. But Catholics would defend him, if they chose to do so, from another viewpoint. They would say that he *could* have been sincere in his decision to avoid having children of the marriage!

Now, anyone but a Catholic would find this hard to take seriously, but Catholic thinking has to take all possibilities into account. This is the high point of the whole controversy. The sacrament may be wrongly entered into, yet it can hold good; provided that it has been invoked by the right solemnisation of vows. On the other hand it may be rightly entered into, but worthless.

For most non-Catholics, such a complexity of morals is enough to defy understanding, but a subtler justice prevails in Catholic courts. There, the coupling of sacrament to intention, of God's blessing to actual bond in law, is exhaustively questioned. A particular case is often quoted by canon lawyers, and from it can clearly be seen the need for careful consideration.

A woman who had made her husband agree to use contraceptives from the start of their marriage, once brought a plea to the Rota for a nullity decree which was forced to endure four hearings. The first decision of the Rota came four years and three months before the final decision of the Supreme Signatura. Two of the verdicts were positive; two were negative, but the final judgement was for nullity.

What, one wonders, can have balanced the legal issue of this case on such a fine point of argument? The woman had, admittedly, entered the marriage somewhat reluctantly. She had been persuaded to go through with it, but after only five months the couple had separated. They were divorced civilly a year later, and it was ten years before the husband approached his priest.

When the case came to the marriage courts the ground on which they were asked to decide was that the wife had 'excluded the essential right and obligation, as regards procreation, from the marriage contract'. The major question was the woman's determination to bar the way to procreation *indefinitely*. Had she insisted on the use of birth control for a period of time only?

If there had been a firm agreement with her husband *never* to 'fulfil her obligation', then the court would have been justified in granting annulment. The first court held this not to have been the case. Their decision was negative. But at the second trial the court could find no evidence of any limit having been set upon the woman's restriction. The decision was reversed, and the case crawled wearily on towards its final verdict. That is, it *would* have been a final verdict—if it had agreed with the previous decision. But concordant judgements must be consecutive, and the third trial held the marriage good, for the same reason that the first had done.

So, a fourth gathering of evidence, another sifting of testimonies and hearing of witnesses, had to be undergone. As a lawyer explained during the first hearing: 'The purpose not to have children must be scrutinised to determine whether the obligation and rights were excluded, or only their fulfilment and exercise.' This was the crux of this important case. It was to be noted that the Rota held to a conviction, implicit in English law, that the person accused is innocent until proved guilty. In this case, the woman said to have insisted on using contraceptives was—under the judge's order—'generally presumed' to have excluded only the fulfilment of the obligation until the contrary was proved.

It *was* proved, and the deprived husband was able to seek another wife, but whether the establishment of legal precedent had been at the cost of two people's happiness is another matter. Any case as personal as this must weigh heavily on the hearts and minds of those intimately involved. This couple had to stand the strain of four long, exhausting hearings. Fortunately, the result finally swung in their favour, but there had never been any guarantee of such ultimate success.

A curious use of this same ground of excluding children from a marriage was seen in another case. This was where the Rota annulled the marriage of a man whose wife had refused to share his bed. It seems that she had married while in love with someone else; and she went back to her lover as soon as the wedding ceremony with her husband was over. Lacking desertion as a cause of divorce, the diocesan marriage court tried this case on two counts— simulated consent, which can be a cause of nullity, and exclusion of procreation. It was the latter which won the case for the deserted and cuckolded husband.

Because of his wife's refusal he had been prevented from enjoying his marital right to father her children. Hence the *obligation* as well as the *fulfilment* of it had been withheld. Or had it? Presumably the woman might have relented, and returned to her rightful husband in time. She might indeed have claimed that that was her intention.

Had she declared that her sinful desertion was merely an impulsive and uncontrollable act, which she was now anxious to put right, it is more than doubtful whether the husband would have won. And if she did *not* intend to return to him one day, it is difficult to understand why she married him at all.

The courts of marriage secrets are filled with similar surprises. Many are due to shades of meaning. But there are also some astonishing facts. In the Catholic courts a woman who has given birth to her husband's children during their marriage can still sue him for non-consummation of her marriage. Equally, a mother may petition the Rota on the grounds of exclusion of children, and this has occurred more than once.

The birth of a child, or children, to such women is not thought to be an insurmountable barrier. We have the case of Mrs Y to prove it. She received a nullity decree from the Rota. During her marriage she had had an abortion, and subsequently she actually bore a child of the marriage. But all this was disregarded by the court. The woman's plea was that she had always been against having children. She had written several letters—which she produced—to various witnesses, both before and during her marriage, indicating this state of mind, and she had consistently opposed her husband's wish to have a family.

It took three long-drawn out trials to uphold the first nullity verdict. The second court suspected collusion between the parties, and reversed the decision. Eventually it was sustained. The mother who had twice been pregnant against her will was freed to marry someone with whom she might not feel so ill-disposed to join in the full sacramental vow of marriage.

Another tragic suit succeeded when a Catholic woman married a man infected with syphilis. The Defender claimed that the couple's agreement never to have children, as they were afraid of the possible effect of the disease on them, was not necessarily binding. The husband, he said, might recover, and the agreement could then be put aside, and a family born of the union. The judges maintained otherwise. Their decision was that the marriage was null and void.

In this case the obligation as well as the fulfilment of the obligation was proved to have been prevented. The disease was such, said the court, that the woman would never have felt safe in bearing her husband's offspring throughout their life together, not even if he had been fully cured. It is this question of obligation and its fulfilment which dominates these cases of exclusion of children. But occasionally there is a flash of originality in the court's attitude to the intention alleged.

Some years ago, the Rota granted annulment to a man who had been 'inane' enough to study the teachings of Nietzsche. An atheist and philosopher, he had refused utterly to consider having children in his marriage, and his wife accepted the condition. The Church, having no reason to deny that, on the evidence, his irreligious attitude was unshakeable and lasting, granted the nullity.

Two years before this verdict, the Rota had decided a case which involved the very poignant question of a wife's ability to bear children without losing her own life in the process. Without hesitation, the tribunal declared null the marriage of a girl whose weak heart had made child-bearing dangerous, so that her husband and she had agreed not to attempt a family. For such a condition, which in non-Catholic eyes might seem to over-rule all other considerations, is not automatically held by Catholics to alter the blessed purpose of marriage.

Another conundrum lies in the meaning of the absolute indissolubility of a marriage. We have noted that this can affect a plea of faulty intention. At close quarters it differs considerably from the exclusion of children, for we know Roman Catholics believe that marriage is indissoluble by man; not that it *may* be, or *can* be, or *ought* to be, but that it is.

Therefore the marriage behaviour of all baptised Christians comes under this ruling in Catholic eyes. Those non-Catholics who undo their marriages by divorce and other means are in the Roman Church's opinion making a mistake. But they are in *simplex error* only, to use the legal term.

Two Presbyterians discovered this to their cost some years ago. They had married in a Register Office and then subsequently re-married in their Church. In neither case did their vows exclude possible dissolubility. The religious ceremony had included the words 'till death do us part'. Otherwise it had differed little from the civil ceremony. The Presbyterian Church, in common with most other non-Catholic Christian Churches, does not hold its vows above those of the State and its machinery of law.

So the two marriages did not bind the parties to stay married for ever. But, equally, they could not be expected to know that marriage was an unbreakable contract. In this case the man divorced his wife seventeen years after they were married. He then sought to marry a Catholic girl, and, of course, he found his way barred. In the eyes of Rome, he was and had been a married man. Persisting that he was not, he brought his case to the Rota. His plea was that his first marriage was nullified by his intention *at the time it was made* not to respect the indissolubility of the match.

Not so, said the judges. In the first case, baptised Christians who are ignorant of the true nature of marriage cannot have a false intention regarding its inviolacy. Secondly, although the Presbyterian petitioner brought evidence to show that he had resisted the vows of his church wedding, in which he was asked to swear that he would remain wedded to his wife until death parted them, this had not been before but after he had been properly married by civil law. The Church of Rome recognises civil marriages among all baptised Christians as valid.

It takes mental juggling to comprehend the legal interpretation here, but it is worth attempting. The Church of Rome has declared itself absolute in terms of its own flock. For them to marry and later divorce is impossible. Equally, they may not marry *with the intention of* later divorcing, because this means that they do not marry at all. Thus they are in no doubt about their situation.

But non-Catholic Christians, says Rome, marry with their eyes and senses blinded to the truth, which is that marriages are for ever, and that no man can put them asunder. He or she does not have a false intention regarding the durability of the union simply because of the type of vow, or understanding of the vow.

If, on the other hand, a separate and positive agreement is made between the non-Catholic Christian parties, that they do not intend their marriage to last, or necessarily to last, then they are no longer in *simplex error*. They must be judged by the full severity of canon law. They *did* intend to exclude the indissolubility of their marriage. Their marriage was therefore null. Though this is unlikely to make sense to anybody but a lawyer, and a lawyer trained in the intricacies of canon law especially, it is the logical reasoning and argument of the Rota on this delicate point. A Catholic who wishes to marry a divorced non-Catholic Christian may make practical use of it.

By asking his intended spouse whether she ever discussed the question of marriage durability with her previous husband before their marriage, he may learn something to his advantage. If she had, and if they had said something like 'Oh, well, if the worst happens we can always get a divorce,' then the way is clear. Prove this, and the court of Rome must concede that it was a form of explicit agreement, contracting not to abide by the indissolubility of marriage.

The tangled skeins of Roman canon law in this are no different from those of Britain and the USA. All contain confusing prolixities. But the dispute is far more intricate where two separate arms of the Christian faith differ on marriage than on many other matters of faith. And among Catholics there are curious anomalies.

Where a Roman Catholic girl has made her prospective husband agree to end their marriage should they be unhappy, provided there are no children, the Rota has often agreed that she is subsequently free. That is to say the Court has proved it has never been a marriage. Yet the question lingers over such decisions: how long had the sacrament of marriage *not* existed?

In one particular case on record the judges admitted that the agreement to marry had been conditional. Hence, had a child been born of the marriage it would, on the face of it, have invalidated the agreement. Presumably, the wife could then have gone on living with the husband she no longer loved. *But would she have been married to him?* Remember that marriage knots are not untied by the Rota, they are merely judged never to have been tied.

In this case, the knot (i.e. the sacrament) was absent from the time when the girl failed to accept the marriage under the terms of her agreement. But, as she had previously said, its existence depended on her having a child. Would she and her husband then have been living in sin if they had gone on living together? Would the Church have judged their marriage invalid? No, because the intention to divorce would then have been revoked, and this action would have shown that it was only a temporary, and not a lasting, impediment. The marriage would have been declared sound, since it had been properly made, and it would have existed irrevocably from then onward.

So if any Catholic wants to marry with a cynical built-in insurance against having to stay married, should things not work out too well, this is surely an easy way to do it. It is the perfect way out, and many sophisticated Romans use it. All that any prospective bride or groom needs is a similar agreement. Provided there are no children, the marriage courts will almost certainly allow that there was 'faulty intention'.

This is not intended as gratuitous advice on how to break ecclesiastical and moral laws. Nor is it based on disrespect for the Church. Such callous evasions of the true principles of matrimony as those suggested above are to be abhorred, no doubt. But if they choose to do so, I am saying, Roman Catholics can defy the best efforts of the courts. The Defenders of Marriage Bonds and all other officers, priests and others are powerless to prove that their marriages are forever.

ELEVEN

A Gilded Cage

The century's most sensational nullity case began its hearing before the Rota on 29th July 1926. Consuela Vanderbilt, daughter of an enormously wealthy American family, claimed that her marriage to one of England's most illustrious aristocrats, Charles, Duke of Marlborough, had been forced on her by an ambitious mother.

In many ways the suit was sadder and more revealing than any heard by the celibate tribunals of the marriage courts in recent years. Also, it evoked more rumour, and it brought odium of the Church of Rome. Throughout the long period of the hearings Catholics were obliged to defend their courts against bitter attack. Why, people asked, was the suit being heard *more than a quarter of a century after the marriage*? There were other and uglier questions. Prejudiced outsiders suggested that the required verdict was being 'bought'. How else, they asked, could a marriage which had produced two children, and lasted so long, be proved not to have existed?

When the decision came—'nullity granted'—the torrent of scorn provoked by it was withering. At its core was the knowledge that both parties had already been divorced, and both had remarried. Now they had had their marriage swept aside like so many crumbs. *And Consuela was not even a Catholic*. To a world being allowed a rare glimpse of the workings of the Roman marriage court, this seemed an incredible piece of ecclesiastical jiggery-pokery. The Duchess had pleaded with tragic intensity. The sadness of her story was undeniable. But what were the facts? If Consuela's marriage could have been sustained while she bore the Duke's children, how could she now say that it had been only a pretence?

The story as it unfolded in intimate detail before the court was in many ways a classic tragedy. Here was a beautiful young heiress torn from her lover by the overbearing design of her mother on an English dukedom. In fiction or drama, such a tragedy would rarely have failed to palpitate the human heart. But in her lonely bedroom it was of far more real tragedy to the seventeen-year-old girl who sat at its heart. Consuela made a poignant heroine. The bars of her cage were no less restricting because they were made of gold.

Her lover, the Rota reported, was 'a certain man by name M . . . R . . .'. We are allowed no more knowledge of him than that. The great names could be bandied about. His remains undisclosed. It can be assumed that he was richer in those qualities liable to stir the heart of a romantic young girl than in the rank, title and other material possessions for which Consuela's mother had so profound a regard.

Mrs Vanderbilt had made up her mind about this. Her daughter was not going to throw herself away. Thus the lovers' problems can easily be imagined. The beautiful Consuela's home was a great mansion at Newport, the palatial seat of the Vanderbilts. For her it became an unassailable fortress, imprisoning her heart amid sighs and languishings. The hot-blooded young man she loved met her whenever possible under a cloak of enormous secrecy. Both knew their love was doomed, but young lovers would not be what they are if they did not sometimes strive for the moon.

Consuela and M . . . R . . . became secretly engaged, and the girl faced her mother declaring she would 'wed no other'. Mrs Vanderbilt grew more determined. Consuela's passion was ridiculed as a flight of girlish fancy, an infection as transient as hay-fever. The chilly history of the case depicts the mother's attitude of mind in distressing clarity: 'As Consuela was a girl,' it observed, 'who possessed both youth, beauty, a great future and a brilliant education, she (the mother) intended to betroth her only to the flower of English nobility.'

No ambiguity existed in this plan. Consuela was to be sold on the marriage market of her time, in common with royal princesses and other ladies of great wealth and standing. Her value, in her ambitious mother's eyes, could merit no less. It was in order to achieve this that Mrs Vanderbilt had allowed herself to be introduced to Charles, Duke of Marlborough, in London. He had been speedily invited to be her guest at her home near the sea, so adjacent to all those other Americans of wealth and distinction who composed the 'Newport set'.

Poor Consuela! She may have been glad even of this respite from her mother's intentions. Since her mother's declaration at Newport, the girl's private world had become a torture chamber. She was ordered to avoid all future contact with the young man she loved. To ensure this, Mrs Vanderbilt packed her off immediately for a European holiday. Thus the final snaring of her mother's quarry came as a relief from the chase. Now, at least, they could return home to be near her adored M.

A smuggled letter, bearing a London postmark, told him the news. Vain hopes were exchanged. How pitifully an emancipated and unfeeling generation was to look back on this tragedy four decades later, when three chaste priests would expose the musty *pot-pourri* of its memory!

At the time the young couple's vows were stronger than

all the demands of a designing world. Love blinded them. Even the Roman court was later to sympathise with their situation. 'The mother,' said the pronouncement of the judges, 'stubbornly refused to endorse her daughter's wishes. Solely in order to destroy the love in the heart of the girl, she had taken her to Europe.'

The long sea journey home proved only an additional torment. Consuela now had to endure her mother's constant companionship, and whenever they were together, Mrs Vanderbilt would turn the conversation round to the subject of the Duke and his many virtues. She let drop broad hints of the future prospects, not to mention good fortune, of a girl who would become his bride. Consuela had to listen patiently. It was noticed that at mealtimes she crumbled her bread on the tablecloth with every sign of frustration and helplessness.

Whatever she had planned was subtly outmanœuvred by her mother. Such allies as she had within her family circle were stripped of their power to help Consuela by superior strategies, and in September the Duke arrived from England.

We can be sure that he was well aware of the business aspects of his visit: an exchange of desirable wealth was to be made for eligible rank and title. Whether he loved Consuela or not, the motives of her mother must have been clearly discernible to Charles, Duke of Marlborough, master of Blenheim Palace, and a descendant of one of England's noblest heroes.

But his arrival was not auspicious, as witnessed the pale face and lack-lustre eyes of the young girl who was to become his property in marriage. However hard Consuela tried to obey her mother's wishes—that she should 'disport herself as a young lady' and not give way to an impulse to hurl her mother's delicate china tea service at his head—it was not possible to do this to the letter.

As she was to tell the court, in one of her most tragic descriptions of the forces which drove her finally to submit: 'My mother cut off all my contact with my suitor. She forced me to leave my country, intercepted all letters which he wrote to me, and I to him. She made continual scenes.

'She told me that I must obey her; that she was convinced that I had no right to make a choice in marriage, that I must accept the man *she* chose, and that my refusal to do so was destroying her health and would probably cause her death.

'There was one terrible scene when she told me that if I succeeded in running away from her [as Consuela had threatened to do] she would seize the first opportunity to shoot my lover, and then she would be sent to prison and hanged, and *I* would be responsible!'

In spite of her disciplined up-bringing, that autumn visit of the Duke's crushed Consuela's spirit. Marlborough's attitude towards her—towards the whole business, in fact—seemed to be one of bored condescension. In a heartrending passage delivered by her lawyer, Consuela showed her feeling for this man thrust on her as a husband. 'His arrogance forced me to regard him as an enemy,' she said. 'He had the air of despising everything not English, and, oh, how this rankled against my American pride!' But she could not escape him. Mrs Vanderbilt was an active stage-manager, and she arranged a succession of meetings between them.

Both knew the purpose of these encounters. The Duke, aloof and reserved, looking down on this pale girl, whose wild eyes never accorded with the smile so politely forced to her lips. Ah, these Americans! his expression seemed to say . . . what a lot they still have to learn!

To Consuela the nightmare was barely endurable. She found the dreadful 'command attendances' demanded by her mother a mounting torture. The balls, parties and tea-

times moved across her mental vision in an unending series
of ordeals. Indeed, the very home which she had grown up
to know and love had become a rack on which she was
increasingly stretched. M had been banished. He could no
longer even approach his beloved. Against one of the most
powerful rivals in the world, what chance had this plain
American?

On the evening before his departure, the Duke made a
proposal of marriage. Would Consuela be his duchess?
Would she be mistress of Blenheim? Her reply was
unnecessary, for Consuela's mother had already given her
consent. The announcement of the betrothal had been sent
to the newspapers before the Duke opened his mouth. The
thought that her wishes could be denied had been unthinkable to Mrs Vanderbilt.

At least a flicker of Consuela's feelings must have been
apparent to her fiancé. In supporting her annulment plea
the Duke later said: 'She told me that her mother had
insisted that she should marry me, that her mother was
fiercely opposed to her marriage with M R, and that all
constraint, almost to the extent of physical violence, had
been used to achieve these ends . . .' Yet he did nothing to
protect the young girl he professed to love from this out-
rageous pressure.

The Duke, presumably, was worldly enough to accept the
fact that marriages are *not* always made in heaven, that
many people in high places have far less attraction for their
partners than is popularly believed, and that this is an
inevitable part of life at the pinnacle of power and wealth.

The tragedy of Consuela Vanderbilt was consummated at
their wedding, in a Protestant Church in New York, some
six weeks after the Duke's proposal. In the Rota report, we
see a brief and dispassionate account of what followed:
'Now this marriage,' it says in its antiquated Latin, 'had
an unfortunate outcome. For a short time after it had

been made, the wife told the husband that she had gone to the altar unwillingly, and only under compulsion from her mother. She still burned with love for another man.

'This brought a separation of mind, and the wife gravely neglected the Duke. After two children had been born of the marriage (following *ten years* of marriage), the spouses separated as regards bed and cohabitation.

'After *twenty five* years together they obtained a civil divorce by mutual consent, but five years later the woman petitioned the Diocesan Court of Southwark for a declaration of nullity of her marriage with Charles, and, the due procedure having been completed, a judgement was given of nullity of marriage on the grounds of fear and force.

'The Defender of the Bond appealed to this Holy Rota, and the case now comes under consideration in the form of the doubt "Does nullity of marriage exist in this case?" '

The answer, as a fascinated world was astonished to learn, was that it did. Some *forty one* years after this unhappy couple had been wed, and after they had both (though neither of them Catholics at the time) committed the 'mortal sin' of divorcing and re-marrying others, their union was found never to have received the divine sacrament. Never, in fact, to have occurred at all.

The relief to Consuela may have been immense. It could hardly make up for the torture she had been subjected to as the unknowing victim of this entire machination. How much simpler everything would have been *had she only been a Roman Catholic in the beginning*!

For the legal position was unusually straightforward in her case. Once it could be proved that force, resulting in fear, had dictated the marriage consent, then the marriage was a mere contrivance. It had no spiritual value in the law of the Church of Rome. So, if the persuasion by Mrs Vanderbilt was *proved* to have amounted to 'grave force', it automatically rendered the marriage invalid.

All who gave testimony in the final hearing agreed that such forceful persuasion had existed, that the tragic Consuela's matrimonial life, including ten years spent as Marlborough's wife and the bearing of two children to him, had occurred solely out of obedience to her mother. If any shred of doubt lingered, this evidence resolved it. There was the testimony of an aunt: 'This marriage was imposed by my sister on her daughter who, as I have already said, wished to marry someone else.'

Another witness, Mrs Lucia Jay, was asked outright by the judge: 'Do you believe that the pressure here was simple persuasion, or what could amount to coercion?' She declared, on oath before the Rota: 'It was not persuasion, but absolute coercion. I swear it, I know it!'

Even Mrs Vanderbilt finally admitted: 'I *did* force my daughter to marry the Duke. I have always had complete authority over her. My children were solely entrusted to my care after my divorce and I, and I alone, was responsible for their upbringing.'

She continued: 'When I gave a command, not one of them dared to contradict me. For this reason I did not *ask* her or implore her to marry the Duke. I simply commanded her to do so.'

Consuela's mother ended her story with these words: 'When I invited the Duke to visit me at my home in Newport, he came and stayed about a fortnight. Then I told my daughter he was the man I had chosen to be her husband. She was terribly upset. She insisted that she could not marry him. But I considered that I was justified in ignoring her opposition, as merely the foolishness of an inexperienced young girl.'

Compare these impassioned statements with the cold

indifference shown during Consuela's fight to marry the man she loved. In public, the wide disparity was not over-looked. Doubts were felt by many Roman Catholics as a result of this case.

The Rota had judged an assembly of legal facts. But were these facts—despite the solemn oaths under which they had been submitted—true to the actual conditions of the marriage as it had occurred? The court had been powerless to question them. It had only power to request witnesses to reiterate what they had sworn. Since no cross-examination is possible, the tricks of civil lawyers are absent from these hearings. But so is the effective issue.

As a result, suspicion has grown that the Vanderbilts and the Marlboroughs employed their money and position to good advantage in this case; at the very least these privileges gave them the finest and most skilled advisers in drawing up Consuela's plea.

Ultimately, a learned trio of canon judges faced what was a clear-cut case. 'There is very little doubt,' they declared, 'as to the gravity of the fear. Assuming that it is possible for grave fear to exist without threats and blows, and that the indignation of parents can at once be an evil and a grave evil. . . .'

The assumption was corroborated on all sides.

The court concluded: 'If the papers are examined, we see that the gravity of the fear is conclusively demonstrated. All the witnesses state that the girl married Charles when overcome by the irresistible will of her mother. It is to be remembered that she was in the habit of trembling in her mother's presence—she, who was sweet, and gentle, and accustomed to obey, whereas the mother was imperious when opposed. She was accustomed to going against people and to subjecting everything to her own ideas and her uncontrollable will.'

The court then revealed: 'Unless she married Charles,

Consuela had to fear another grave danger, namely, the death of her mother. We have this on the opinion of her doctor. It was a point which the mother used frequently as a threat. Consuela has told us: "My mother told me several times that if I persisted in opposing her wishes it would be so upsetting to her that, in view of her health, it could well cause her death. This too, was the opinion of her doctors!" '

Finally the Rota judges declared: 'This sworn assertion was confirmed by an aunt: "My sister made continual scenes with her daughter, and tried to win her over by telling her that she had a weak heart and, if Consuela continued to resist her, she would die." '

Even so, the court recognised that Consuela too could be rebellious: 'Notwithstanding all this,' the judges declared, 'Consuela did not wholly fall in with her mother's wishes. This becomes clear from the fact that when the man (Marlborough) asked her to marry him, she gave no consent but shed tears. But she read of the engagement in the following day's papers, *despite* her lack of agreement.

'In short, having no one to turn to, when the threats did not cease and the mother's decision remained inflexible, Consuela at last entered into wedlock with Charles. The truth is that Consuela had been compelled to choose marriage to escape from fear.'

If the judges needed further proof, they had it in abundance. When Consuela had finally agreed, Mrs Vanderbilt had suspected a ruse. She had had a sentry posted at her daughter's bedroom door so that nobody was allowed to come to her room, day or night, and talk to her.

Consuela became a prisoner for the five weeks or so of her future husband's absence, during which time Charles toured Canada and prepared himself for the inevitable, if tiresome, necessity of marriage. Nobody was surprised when he later told the court: 'My wife arrived very late for our wedding, and appeared troubled.' The astonishing fact is that she arrived at all.

Could Consuela have failed in her plea? It is possible. Had she *known* that her marriage was not a true and sacramental bond, then by continuing to live with the Duke during their early married years she might have ruined her case. In Catholic canon law, such behaviour constitutes ratification. But Consuela could not have had knowledge of ecclesiastical, or canon, law. In these, by quaint definition, 'women are not to be presumed to have any such knowledge'.

So, with comfortable blandness, the Rota were able to declare: 'Since in this case no proofs appear of any knowledge of the invalidating implement, and since the mental separation set in very shortly after the celebration of the marriage, and lasted till the divorce judgement, it cannot be pretended that there was any renewal of consent on the part of Consuela.'

From their point of view, this removed all obstacles. 'Having considered all these things and weighed them carefully, calling upon the name of Christ,' declared the three judges solemnly, 'we the undersigned Auditors forming this tribunal and answerable only to God for our action, confirm the decision of the Court of Southwark and declare and finally decide that "the nullity of the marriage between Consuela Vanderbilt and Charles Marlborough is proved".

'Thus we reply, to the doubt proposed, "affirmative". And we decree that the said Consuela Vanderbilt shall be responsible for all the expenses involved in this trial.

'Given at Rome, at the offices of the Court of the Holy Roman Rota on the 29th July 1926.'

Rome was satisfied. The Church had expressed its absolute conviction, grounded in canon law, that no marriage had ever existed between these two. Only a doubting world continued to ask questions about this non-marriage of a couple who seemed, on the face of it, to have used the laws of Church and State to suit their own richly-bound books.

Neither the Rota nor the Church's highest officers felt in the least doubtful about this issue, nor was it a case of such complexity and legal obscurity that it had to be wrapped in secrecy for fear of gross misunderstanding—as in the Radziwill case. But the criticism persists.

Had Consuela and Charles been Catholics, married in a Catholic church, the opportunity for this nullity might never have occurred. But they were not. What continues to bother doubting non-Catholics is that these two, rich, powerful families were able to use first one set of laws and then another to gain their ends. The Vanderbilts and the Marlboroughs came well out of it. Only two persons, it seems, were permanently harmed: Consuela Vanderbilt and her unrequited fiancé, M . . . R . . . Neither Church nor State could put back the clock for them.

TWELVE

The Critics

With ecumenicism in the air, many non-Catholics are increasingly restive about the Catholic Church's unbending laws, feeling that a sect which finds it necessary to apply such strict rules in such extreme secrecy must, in fact, have plenty to hide. Alone, these alien voices would hardly disturb Rome's conscience. But if we consider the application of the Church's laws of marriage, as against their validity, then we must number a proportion of Catholics among the critics. Both secrecy and delay are increasingly angering those who have dealings with the marriage courts, and the grumble of discontent within the Church grows steadily.

In Britain, a small man with grave eyes and a dry rebellious wit has become a noteworthy leader of this faction. He is a Jesuit, Archbishop Thomas d'Esterre Roberts, trained in argument and steeped in his Church's history and law. Some of his criticisms have hit hard and cut deep.

During the war Roberts held the important post of Catholic Bishop of the British Forces. He was also Bishop of Bombay. When I met him he was at the fashionable R.C. church in Farm Street, Mayfair. His name, I found, had only to be mentioned in Rome to produce a pantomime of long faces and a chorus of murmured disapproval, if only for the reason that Archbishop Roberts's views on the possible future battleground of marriage are of the utmost importance.

We discussed them on a cold, fresh, March morning when his thoughts were divided between our talk and a trip he was about to make abroad. In the small room there was a smell of boiled cabbage, an ashtray spilled butts on to a dusty table, and stained linoleum covered the floor. It was, I thought, a typical background of all Catholic residences where no woman ever has control. A crucifix hung on the wall. Roberts glanced at it somewhat quizzically, I thought, as he spoke of his early experience as a bishop when his diocese had included a marriage court.

It was immediately evident that he had a profound respect for the canon laws governing marriage, however radical his opposition was to their application by his colleagues in the Roman hierarchy. What he outspokenly condemned were certain aspects of the marriage courts: 'Any Englishman brought up in the Church,' he told me, 'is bound to resent canonised secrecy—I might almost call it "divinised" secrecy—which has become such a fetish. I personally believe it is a great mistake.'

This English archbishop, who is also a great believer in internationalising the Church, explained: 'In the Rota many of the important, tried legal systems of other nations are practically unrepresented. Far too many of the judges are Italian, so naturally a parochial view tends to be taken.'

From the author whose book, *Black Popes* (Longmans, Green), stirred the Church to its foundations when published fifteen or so years ago, this was hardly a new theme. Roberts wrote then: 'Today the sanctity of marriage is the real battleground between Christ and the world. Marriage being God's foundation for the family and for the ideal of fatherhood on which our Lord stakes everything.'

Roberts also wrote in this book: 'Fidelity to our Lord's institution of marriage as indissoluble (so excluding divorce) and chaste (so excluding artificial birth-prevention) demands on occasion really heroic holiness. With increasing frequency, conflict is set up between Christian law and civil law. To resolve such conflicts is one reason why the Church has her own courts. They exist by divine right; equally by divine obligation they ought to be models to the world of what a court should be. . . .'

Archbishop Roberts smiled when I reminded him of these words of his. He told me: 'Having travelled widely I have heard much of these courts. What I have found in general is a very strong criticism of incompetence and delays. In practice, a devout Catholic may be bearing cheerfully the cross imposed by the law of Christ. But how can he bear what is frequently imposed by the courts? These additional torments, such as years of delay, are certainly not of Christ's making.'

In his book, he had added, 'It seems necessary to add that everything said here in criticism of matrimonial court procedure has been said by the author to His Holiness the Pope at a private audience.' In fact, as Roberts confirmed, a test marriage case was once brought by him, and a solution given in view of the urgency, only two days afterwards. 'Through the ordinary channels,' he explained, 'it might have taken several years.'

Archbishop Roberts's face lit up with innocent joy as he described this case, which occurred in 1945, to me. 'I got the RAF to fly me to Rome,' he explained. 'There, I saw Pius XII, whom I knew well, and told him the facts of the case . . . the urgency of it. The girl's position was dreadful, she had waited patiently for so long. And when I'd done, I could see that the Pope was very impressed. He told me: "You can consult any three priests of the Gregorian University here in Rome, and on their word of recommendation alone I will grant the dissolution." '

Archbishop Roberts's eyes twinkled. 'It was unheard of, but I knew Pius liked doing things on his own. I had banked on that, and it came off. I got the case settled inside three days . . . yet I have known cases to take ten years!'

This figure has been strongly challenged. When Archbishop Roberts reportedly stated it at a press conference in Rome, during the Council in October 1963, Canon W. P. Denning of Southwark commented in a letter to the English newspaper, *The Catholic Herald*: 'Having read . . . that Archbishop Roberts told a press conference in Rome that it normally takes ten years to obtain from Rome the dissolution of an unconsummated marriage, I have been through my files relating to Southwark cases of this kind decided during the last three years. The results are as follows:

Case	Date when petitioner was notified of dissolution			Year when case was introduced to Southwark
A	Jan	3	'61	1958
B	Feb	2	'61	1959
C	June	27	'61	1959
D	July	20	'62	1959
E	Feb	1	'62	1959
F	June	14	'62	1959
G	Sep	6	'62	1960
H	Feb	21	'63	1958
I	June	20	'63	1960
J	July	20	'63	1961
K	Sep	5	'63	1961

'I am confident that most curias in this country would produce similar figures, and that almost all those who work on matrimonial cases both in this country and in Rome are conscious of their duty to reduce delays to a minimum. There is still of course room for improvement, but it would be a pity if petitioners and their advisers were discouraged by His Grace's statement.'

Roberts's reply was typical: 'Any Christian (or even rational) inquisition,' he wrote to the same paper, 'seeks not only to enquire and reform, but also to disclose the sources of inspiration. Let us hope that other English curias (we are concerned at the Council with all the world's curias) will produce—as the Canon thinks they could—similar figures. But only a very frank enquiry will disclose (1) What degree of confidence in our courts does in fact exist. (2) What measures must be taken to secure the improvement admitted by Canon Denning as desirable.'

Silence greeted this. But inside the Church the seeds of revolt were being scattered by the Archbishop's candid blast at Rome's delays and secrecy. In March 1964, when the announcement of Princess Caroline Lee Radziwill's marital nullification was made from Rome, the first shoots appeared. 'As is usual,' wrote the editor of *The Catholic Herald* tartly, 'the reason for the annulment is not disclosed.' Elsewhere, the same paper was commenting: 'Whether the parties are rich or poor, many of these matrimonial cases take a very long time, and many are rejected after exhaustive enquiry. Bitter complaints have been made by some bishops about the delays. We know of one influential Catholic who had to wait twelve years. Even the Princess waited for four.'

The paper continued: 'The Roman Rota is a stern tribunal bent on establishing truth, demanding higher standards than the balance of probabilities acceptable in civil courts here. Its judges are extremely hard-working men with first-class minds. They may tell you privately that the bottle-necks are the fault of the diocesan courts, not the Rota. In return, the local courts accuse the Rota of archaic secretarial methods, urgently needing overhaul. These judges are very tough nuts to crack. . . .'

After this thunder-clap the storm quickly grew. An assistant priest of an English Roman Catholic church at Perivale wrote to the paper: 'Ecclesiastical officialdom has seen fit to shroud the whole affair with a "no comment" blanket of silence. We are not told whether, since the Radziwills seem to have taken the law into their own hands and "married" four years ago in a civil ceremony "not recognised by the Church", they were excommunicated, and, since the decision of the Rota, whether they have been restored to communion and reconciled with the Church!'

The point was well made. The same writer continued: 'Coming at a time when we are trying to understand one another, particularly with regard to the problem of so-called mixed marriage, this incident does, at any rate to a non-Roman Catholic, make arrant nonsense of so many of the arguments put forward on this subject, more especially since, in this case, there appears to have been a succession of "husbands and wives".'

This English priest concluded: 'It does seem unfortunate to me that this sort of thing is allowed to happen, without any apparent comment or censure from those in a position to do so. It can only do untold harm to the cause of Christian Unity, apart from complicating the work of many a poor priest who has to try and explain to his bewildered flock the sacred state of Holy Matrimony, whether that priest be of the Roman Obedience or not!'

In reply, and possibly to set the picture straight, the paper published a tangential rebuke from W. J. Ingoe of Loughton, Essex: 'Has it occurred to Father Wills that his suggestion—that the details of such cases be publicised—logically might lead to the installation of loud-speakers on confessionals?' he asked, 'People are entitled, by right of being persons (princesses, by the way *are* persons), to the decent privacy the Rota's method ensures.'

Still the clouds refused to disperse. Writing from Paddington, London, Elizabeth Price joined in: 'The *Magna Carta* principle of justice being seen to be done is applied to divorce in this country. I do not say the public should be allowed to listen to the workings of the Rota, or that intimate and salacious details should go to press. But the general reasons should be published. How simple this would make the task of explaining to the disedified, or answering the jibe that only the rich are favoured!'

The paper allowed the correspondence to die after this. But the point had been made, and with unusual clarity. Catholics, in Britain anyway, were alarmed, frustrated and outraged by the Radziwill case, because it appeared to them to confound all the Church's most stringent teachings, and because every shred of information—barring the final successful conclusion—was withheld, as though the faithful were too young, or too unimportant, to share such weighty secrets.

What was so upsetting about this case? Mainly that Lee Radziwill, whose supposed marriage to publisher Michael Canfield was annulled by it, was the sister-in-law of the president of the USA and also that she had failed to gain a nullity decree *before* her sister's husband, the late John F. Kennedy, had risen to his important post.

It was remembered that in September 1962 Mrs Jacqueline Kennedy had spent a holiday in the Italian village of Ravello with Lee and her husband Stanislas. Radziwill, it appeared, was a man who had already received an annulment of his first marriage with the present Baroness de Chollet, wife of a Swiss banker. His second marriage, with a shipping heiress named Grace Kolin, who had afterwards married the Earl of Dudley (whose ex-wife, Laura Charteris, later married the late Michael Canfield, before he became Lee's first husband), had never been recognised in Rome. This was due, of course, to the unchallenged validity of the first marriage. By the time Radziwill received the nullity decree of this first bond he had already divorced Grace and was about to marry Lee.

Again, it had to be a civil ceremony, but the lack of a Catholic ceremony was not caused by *his* marital situation on this occasion, but by hers. Lee's marriage to Canfield still existed. In the eyes of the Church, until the nullity decree later freed her, she was forced to live with Radziwill in a state regarded by Catholics as mortal and infamous sin.

This highly involved game of not-so-Happy Families, led to a rude suspicion that Lee's nullity attempts, supported by her influential sister, were being given undue consideration in Rome. The number of marriage ceremonies celebrated by Lee and her husband to join them both in Church and State was remarkable. Prior to their Catholic Church wedding, in June 1963, four years had been spent in legal wrangling, several hundred pages of Latin depositions had been prepared, innumerable witnesses had been paraded before the Rota in three hearings, and expenses had been incurred which, I was told by a friend of the family in London, amounted to many thousand pounds.

None of this might have attracted criticism from loyal Catholics had the facts of the case been made known. But the decision was all that was, or ever will be, released of the delicate judgement in the Radziwill case by the Sacred Rota. With customary secrecy, even the late Michael Canfield was excluded from knowledge of the text of the verdict. He was not told the grounds on which his ex-wife's case had been won.

Such secrecy is infrequent but, as we have previously seen, it does occur. The Church claims it is a means of protecting judgements 'from vulgar and unwarranted criticism' but, regrettably, it most frequently seems to be used in cases where great public interest and curiosity have been aroused. Thus it attracts world-wide attention and criticism, and a growing number of Catholics feel that such 'Star Chamber' tactics should cease, if only for the sake of their Church's image.

Another disturbing aspect of the Radziwill suit was that it had the privilege of being heard by the Rota at *first instance*: a procedure so unusual as to be almost unique. This case had already failed (though presumably on different grounds) when instituted in England, in October 1958. Now it received two concordant, affirmative decisions from the highest court in the Church. Any ordinary Catholic would have been heartened by a hint of the reasons for such indulgence by the busy court, especially as the Rota claims to have so little time to spare and its judges complain that they are stretched to the limit. A backlog of six hundred or so cases waiting for attention does not suggest unlimited elbow-room for such special considerations. But in the Radziwill case, as always, the Rota preserved characteristic silence.

While in Rome, I discussed what could be discussed of the case with Princess Lee's distinguished lawyer, Professor Fernando Della Rocca. I was told by this kindly and reputedly brilliant advocate, 'There is nothing I can tell you. The case was protected by a very special secrecy, such as we use at the Rota every so often. We call these cases *speciale sigillio*. They are so secret that an advocate, such as myself, has to swear a solemn oath not to divulge any of the procedure or findings even to the clerks of the Rota, or to the Chancellor, who is the Rotal secretary. In such cases, it is not uncommon for the petitioner to be left in ignorance of the full text of his or her own sentence.'

Why should a lawyer have to swear a *special* oath, when surely his professional standards bind him, one would think, to total secrecy? 'In very delicate cases,' Professor Della Rocca explained, 'we have to swear that we will observe silence on *even more details* than would otherwise seem necessary. This vow limits those with whom one can discuss the case, *even in the circle of one's own legal colleagues*!'

The Rota is not required to explain its demand for such vows of obedience from its advocates. As part of the most rigorous court in the world, its lawyers must accept unusual strictures. There are seventy-five who do so, the canon lawyers qualified to appear in person before its tribunals.

Each has spent at least three years at the *Studio Rotali* law school in Rome, where they will have received special instruction. And this follows, it does not take the place of, normal legal training. So a man must devote many years of his life to reaching the position of *Advocati in tribunali S. R. Rotae*. And not one of these lawyers has ever, publicly, expressed doubts about the wisdom of veiling so much of the court's work in secrecy.

Professor Della Rocca did go so far as to say that he felt 'concerned' about the length of time some cases took to be heard. He had no direct criticism to make of the secretive methods of the court. Yet justification is hard to find for withholding all the facts of a case from the parties in it. Canfield's attitude, when I had discussed it with him, had been one of respectful bewilderment towards the court and its ways. Ignorant of the facts, he was apprehensive that false data could have misrepresented his whole attitude to the marriage, and might—despite every denial—have led to the favourable decision. He had told me: 'Lee assured me that it wasn't, as everyone thought, that I had refused to have children. In fact, she said she was very sorry that that story had got into the press. But she couldn't tell me what the grounds were.'

Mr Canfield added, with evident candour: 'As both Lee and I know, any idea that I had not *wanted* to have children by the marriage was ridiculous.' It might be thought that doubts such as these, in a non-Catholic's mind, should have been instantly dispelled by the Rota, if only in the deepest confidence, but this can never be done. Whereas ordinary cases are published, in a shortened and usually anonymous form, ten years after they have received their verdicts, the specially secret suits are not recorded, except in cryptic, and wholly general, terms. The pity of this is that some of these cases must surely be among the most legally interesting and instructive.

In discussing the Radziwill case with Professor Della Rocca I was told that 'It was my favourite, in twenty-seven years of practice before the Rota. A very exciting case, because there were technical complications during the procedure.' Professor Della Rocca added: 'I overcame many obstacles—the kind which develop when the judge and the Defender of the Bond disagree. The whole case was most fascinating.' But why it was fascinating, neither I nor the student lawyers of the Studio Rotali may ever know in detail.

Such suppression justifies criticism. Yet a far more popular point of attack, hurtful and embarrassing to the lawyers of the Rota, is totally groundless. The advocates do not make huge, personal fortunes out of their work at the Catholic marriage courts. Though many people, both Catholic and non-Catholic, are convinced that 'money can buy a divorce' in Rome, the facts prove otherwise.

Rota lawyers are alone in being allowed to present petitions at the court itself. They are therefore separate and different from the lay, canon advocates who can and do practise in the lower, diocesan courts. Yet they must charge no more for their services in marriage cases than the fees laid down by the Holy Office. I have before me a copy of the scale, or *taxatio proventuum* of these fees printed in 1964. It lists the following:

				Minimum	Maximum
1.	For preliminary study of case and examination of record	Lire Ital.		15,000	30,000
2.	For introducing the case	„	„	5,000	10,000
3.	For instruction	„	„	10,000	40,000
4.	For incidental questioning	„	„	10,000	25,000
5.	For the defence, summing up and replying to oral argument	„	„	40,000	95,000
	Total	„	„	80,000	200,000

At current rates of exchange of 1,500 lire to the pound, these rates do not seem high. They amount to less than many leading attorneys and barristers in Britain charge clients merely for expenses in civil divorce action.

Additionally, the Rota advocates may charge only small, laid-down expenses for such items as 'travelling to a place outside Rome'. The trip must have been made at the request, or with the approval of, the client and with the consent of the Referee (an official of the court).

In fact the rewards, however niggardly, are watched with great care. I was assured by Cardinal Brennan, when Rota Dean, that a very close eye indeed was kept on them. 'There was a wholly inaccurate report in an American paper recently,' he told me, 'saying that a case at the Rota can cost about $5,000 in legal fees! I had to write to the editor about it, but he sent me only a vague reply. We, in fact, are most careful to see that the correct fees are charged. Any advocate found to be charging more than the correct sum would be instantly suspended by us.'

The Dean added: 'Sometimes, of course, mistakes do occur. There *was* a case, just a while ago, when an American in Washington D.C. wrote to ask if he could have his cancelled cheques back—for tax purposes. We discovered then that he had paid out nine thousand dollars to the lawyer! In that instance we took no action because the advocate convinced us that the money had been given out of gratitude, not as a fee.'

These facts and figures, if reliable, show that no fortunes are made from the two hundred cases brought before the Rota each year by up to seventy-five different lawyers. If, in fact, any lawyer secures more than six or eight of these verdicts, his is an exceptional practice. Yet it is these criticisms of high fees, of fortunes being spent on long-drawn-out cases, and of rich clients like the Radziwills being fleeced of enormous costs, that are most often heard about the Rota.

THIRTEEN

Rome Seen, Faith Lost

Beside the gloomy walls of the Pantheon a monk with a modern camera had parked his car and was talking to a beautiful girl. *Roma veduta, fede perduta* (Rome seen, faith lost) said my companion, a Rome journalist, drily. In Rome, it is easy to understand why the world centre of the Catholic religion is widely believed to be one of the least virtuous cities in Europe.

Illegitimacy flourishes. Venereal disease is a constant scourge. There is as much, if not more, sexual licence among teenage Romans as among their counterparts in either Paris or London. I was assured by journalist colleagues that the undisclosed suicide rate is shockingly high, though one experienced Vatican reporter denied this.

Whatever the truth, the outward signs of a national *dolce vita* do exist. They are a constant disturbance to the State's officials. But to the Roman Catholic Church, locked in the hundred and eight acres of the minute Vatican State, and overspilt into a dozen palaces and offices in Rome, the situation is scandalous.

'The paradox, and from the Catholic point of view the tragedy, is that Rome, the centre of Catholicism, is a very ungodly city,' wrote the experienced observer and journalist Corrado Pallenberg in his book *The Vatican from Within* (Harrap).

'When you remember that there are in Rome no less than

1,200 churches, or watch in its streets swarms of priests, monks, friars and nuns, you may think that this is impossible. But if you look at the situation a little more closely, as I have been doing, you see a completely different picture.'

Pallenberg was justified in his criticism. The emptiness of all but a few of the most fashionable churches is evidence of the City's religious indifference. He is right, too, in condemning the ungodliness of a city which is growing increasingly sympathetic to Communism and left-wing Socialism.

Pallenberg pointed out that those who go to church are inclined to treat the place more as a social rendezvous than anything else—a club room where boy meets girl, where women exchange gossip and tittle-tattle, and men discuss the latest football results. At best, he infers, it is somewhere to show-off an ostensible piety, at the same time as displaying the smartest 'status symbol' suits and dresses which Italians so love to parade. The noise of these congregations is astonishing. Often they ignore the chanting of responses and the Mass, while carrying on an animated whispered conversation loud enough to suggest a matinee audience between acts.

There is also a very noticeable lack of communicants in Rome's churches. Even in such 'pagan' countries as Britain one expects to see a fair sprinkling of these at any Catholic High Mass, but here the groups of young girls and old women who generally make up these gatherings at the altar rails are shamefully small. It is Pallenberg's assessment that 'church attendance in Rome is one of the lowest in Italy and in the world'. He reports a growing fear inside the Vatican that municipal administration of the city may soon be in the hands of an amalgamation of Communists and Socialists.

This we have already noted. But how widespread is it? A Catholic journalist in Rome saw this as being beside the point. 'What is one to expect?' he asked. 'A Rome of piety and humility simply because there are 113,000 seminarians studying there? And because Rome has two thousand churches and is the Holy See? *Should* people be kinder and closer to God just because they live where the Church is seated? What about Westminster or Canterbury? Supposing the See had been in Athens or Istanbul?'

He went on to discuss the special difficulties of the Holy City's reputation for commercialism. 'People are just as shocked when they go to Gethsemane or Bethlehem nowadays,' he pointed out. ' "All is so commercial," they say. So many beggars; so much chicanery and thieving. Well, Calvary and Jerusalem have never changed in two thousand years. That is life. That is how it is.'

He added quietly: 'I'm sure when Jesus was dying they were selling *halvah* (sesame) by lamplight just as they do now, and robbing right, left and centre. Rome is like this too. Rome has always been vulgar, teeming, crude, dirty and full of rascals and ragamuffins. It always will be. But I would say that deep down it is no more godless than any other megalopolis.'

What of the hundreds of clerics and friars threading the colourful sidewalks and pavements of the City with sombre flecks of black, purple and brown? Are these avowed servants of Christ doing nothing? The answer seems to be that priests and monks have very little contact with the people of Rome. They are on hand only to serve the Vatican in an official capacity, or to study at one of the universities or seats of learning. They are as incapable of affecting ordinary behaviour as a clerk employed by a government highways department in London or New York would be of preventing road accidents among motorists.

When visiting the capital, they must lead tightly disciplined lives. Orders forbid them to smoke in public. They must not enter a cinema, theatre, sporting arena, or opera house. It is laid down what they must wear, what make of car they may drive, and how much and what sort of television they may watch. This, incidentally must be done *in company with other priests and never alone*.

In Rome, the priests must wear a 'fascia', or belly-band, over their cassock at all times. Even in the extreme heat of high summer this must be worn. They must never accompany a woman alone in a motorcar, and they should not allow themselves to be seen seated *outside* restaurants or cafés except in 'exceptional circumstances'. Pallenberg, in his book, comments sarcastically: 'Presumably when they are either starving or dying of thirst.'

Finally, they must not go without hats or wear anything on their cropped or shaven heads except the regulation round black headgear reminiscent of a nocturnal flying-saucer. It is not so hard to understand why these severely marshalled and governed celibates find it difficult to influence ordinary, café-using, wine-tippling and food-loving Romans. The cynicism of urban Rome seems to be hardening, leading more and more citizens away from the churches.

Even so, is it not better to be nearer God among the pickpockets of Trastevere, or the cheating waiters of Via Vittorio Veneto, than in an Anglican church? A Catholic might well ask this. To a limited extent, too, there may be truth in the Rota judge's complaint who told me: 'We in the Church are very bad about handling our relationships with the public. As far as "image" is concerned, we haven't a clue.'

There is certainly an obstinate reluctance, inside the curia, to bring methods up to date. For many years after airmail was introduced, officials felt suspicious about it. Its use was consequently forbidden. The courts had to send all mail by land and sea, often taking weeks to reach a witness, or lawyer. The Church has always distrusted rapid progress, and where such stubbornness delays a marriage trial it seems hard to defend, bearing in mind the worry and suffering often caused by these interminable trials. To allow them to exist longer than is necessary seems utterly incomprehensible.

In this sense 'Rome seen, faith lost' becomes understandable and real. To enter the courtrooms and offices of the Rota is to join a world where priests live in the past. They must 'clock on' at an ancient time clock each morning, like factory hands, and then work through until midday, when organised work customarily ceases for the day. Many of the judges spend their afternoons and evenings reading and deliberating on the complexities of their cases, although the official working hours of the Sacred Rota are not arduous.

This is the same world that refused, in the period before the eleventh century when scholars were turning to the use of parchment, to desert the far less durable and convenient papyrus of the ancients for their Papal Bulls. It is a world in which electricity is still a mystery, despite power-operated gates and other electronic niceties. At the Vatican Library the lights switch themselves off automatically, on a time switch, every quarter of an hour I was told, to prevent misuse or waste of current. Many find these customs and attitudes charmingly quaint, but if one is to understand why there is such a marked falling off in respect paid to the Church by Roman residents, these are the factors to consider.

Equally important, of course, is the Church's reputation for dealing fairly with vast, contemporary issues. Marriage, birth-control and family-planning are increasingly linked to religious belief in Western society. It is here, above all, that one finds the delicate factors controlling warmth of allegiance to the Roman Church.

A devoted Catholic may declare that 'Annulment is as abhorrent as divorce,' but this can only be the view of those who do not want to be free. To the rest, tolerance is an urgent need. 'It is mostly a problem of the middle classes, the well-to-do bourgeois and his wife,' I was told by a Roman politician. 'It hardly touches the upper or the lower classes, who simply ignore, or cheat, the Church. The bourgeoisie have a conscience—usually a bad one, at that. They want to remain on good terms with the Church, but they want a place in the sunshine also. It is this class of person who is causing the greatest amount of scandal in Italy today.'

The question is whether reform is possible, or whether the surge towards greater moral and social freedom is leading to a split? Rome's finger seems to point to the latter. No priest will accept the likelihood, or even possibility, of a major shift on the marriage issue. Those who disagree are all outside.

'The Church knows,' declared a leading Roman civil lawyer—a man who has advised several petitioners to the Rota—'that something must be done to ease the situation, because they can count: and the number of legal separations which take place in this country is simply enormous. But what is feared is that there will be too many wanting to take advantage of any relaxation in the law, all at once. Personally, I don't share that view, and I think something will be done—will have to be done—fairly soon.'

Explaining his reasons for this forecast, this experienced advocate said: 'Numbers of people in this country have no wish to live as they do, but they are tied to their partners by unions which are *not* marriages. Their children are children of adultery. Either they are the natural children of the woman or, if the man is free, perhaps the natural issue of a "bachelor and a woman not mentioned". They have no right to inherit. Their whole position is grotesque. They are innocent victims of a legal axe.'

These are the notoriously pathetic cases of what are called 'attributed' children. The lawyer went on: 'As our law stands, a married man whose wife has a child by another man has to father that child. He becomes the child's legal parent. Can you imagine anything more repulsive to a husband whose wife has deceived him with another man? But adultery does not provide grounds for divorce, and *something* has to be done about the fruits of it.'

A Rota judge, when interviewed, agreed with this: 'We try to dodge it,' he said. 'Because there is no recipe for it: all that can be done is to leave it to the children's parish priest to talk to them and *advise them*.'

What are the problems of adultery for the parents—at a purely criminal level? In Rome, a man may think he is safely living with somebody else, but his security depends on the silence of his ex-partner, to whom he stays legally married. If she yields to temptation, the prospects for blackmail are enormous. Several thousand better-off Italians are said to pay regular 'insurance' to their legal partners, or agents. The Church may not know the extent of this scandal, but it must be aware that it exists.

If reform is to be brought in by any section of its hierarchy, much will obviously depend on the viewpoint of the supreme pontiff. What does Pope Paul feel should be done? Nobody to whom I have talked believes that he will favour radical changes. Yet he may accept the need for some form of adaptation of fundamental law. His predecessor was known to be moving towards it with outstretched arms.

As an English prelate said with regret: 'Pope John was deliberately trying to open a window. He knew the risks— that a hurricane might come in as well as fresh air—but that did not deter him.'

Others, such as the English Jesuit, Archbishop Roberts, have been equally undeterred by the risks. Writing in a London newspaper in 1964, Roberts gave his view of contraception. He did so as a member of the Vatican Council, and formed a sharp contrast to the opinions of some of his colleagues. It showed where he stood on the whole subject of marriage.

'All my long life,' he wrote, 'I have tried to convince myself [about the validity of the Church's interpretation of God's law regarding marriage] and have quite failed. This could be because I am stupid, or wicked, or both. . . . But of late years, I have had a surprise. Very many clergy and laity, holy and learned, to whom I have confessed my difficulties, have heard them for years. Their sympathy for married Catholics was naturally mixed with some personal fear for themselves. So it occurred to me that if I expressed the thoughts of many, some of them might join me in asking for clarification at the Council. The letters received from priests and people have been a revelation. But there remains the difficulty that even a man as compassionate with the sick and troubled as Archbishop (now Cardinal) Heenan (the article was in answer to a statement by Heenan rejecting "the pill") is, can hold out no hope of release from the brand of mortal sin and of hell fire.'

With significant speed this attack was followed by a searching article in another national newspaper. Mr Martin Legge—described as 'a thinking Catholic who has had experience of social work among Catholic families'—wrote: 'The Roman Catholic Church is made up of millions of married members like myself, as well as the clergy and the Pope. This is not always clear when one is confronted with present-day attitudes within that Church. . . . As others have said before, this is a mess the theologians have got us into and one which they must get us out of, if there is not to be a rift in the Roman Catholic Church. . . .'

The mess he was referring to was the divided view of the prelates on the subject of controlling birth through the oral pill. But the underlying note of rebellion towards the Church's doctrines and dogma offered a hint of the mood of many similarly 'thinking' Catholics.

It is not only in Rome that congregations have been split and confused by the twin problems of their Church's behaviour towards contraception and the dissolution of unwanted marriages. In both the United States and Britain there are priests who will admit to serious concern over these issues. Even in Ireland, where 'the Church right or wrong' has long been a tenet of faith, an increasing number of questions are being asked.

Rome, nevertheless, presents a sad spectacle of rigidity. We have examined the reasons, but the facts remain. Priests and prelates remain distressingly out of touch with modern life. In a Roman lawyer's office I was introduced to a jolly, rotund American Archbishop who reduced a serious conversation to the level of schoolboy larking. He took a small wallet, or folder, from a pocket in his cassock. It was crammed with cheaply jewelled, metallic badges. 'Look,' he cried, 'these are my credentials. They are all my badges of rank!' With jocular insistence he enumerated the various honorary offices—fire chief, mayor's deputy, etc.— to which he had been appointed in his home town. Then he asked me to wet one fingertip with my tongue and place it on a particularly large, glass, ruby set in one of the more ornate of these. 'How would you like to get a holy shock?' he asked playfully. 'Come on—it won't hurt.'

I did as I was asked. And the moment my finger was on the mock stone, the archbishop jerked the badge upwards with a loud bark. 'Bah!' he said, 'Now you have experienced a "holy shock"! How did you like it?' I found it a little hard to reply, while two distinguished canon lawyers and another visitor did their best to appear amused. Perhaps my sense of boyish fun was at fault, but if the Archbishop of Canterbury behaved in such a manner people would doubt, I think, his ability to lead the nation's spiritual welfare.

In Rome, such antics pass unnoticed. As we parted the Archbishop shook hands like a particularly jovial clown.

Then he said loudly:' *Arrivederci* . . . which means I gotta get the hell out-a here!' The expressions of the Italian, but English-speaking, lawyers mirrored some interesting inner conflicts.

Whether this marked frivolity affects the serious reputation of Roman Church officials or not, it is a reflection of an extraordinary ingenuousness. Innocence may sometimes be its own protection against corruption, but it is also a poor attribute when it comes to earning respect in the bourgeois society most damaged by the Church's laws. The bourgeois Catholics judge by their own standards. Italian principles regarding bribery and even corruption are not therefore those which would be acceptable in the City of London. Indeed, many leading Romans have learned that the price of a man is his hidden dimension. Those who fail to offer personal reward for favours done are thought fools.

Even those who pay blackmail are sympathetically admired, and if some of the standards of Rome have rubbed off on the Vatican, who need be surprised? That is not to say that there is evidence of bribe-taking by Church officials, indeed knowledgeable Catholics scorn any such suggestion. Even critics of the Church admit they have never heard a single instance of bribery of a Rota judge or official. But they admit it would be 'out of character' if a Roman petitioner did not 'try it on'. For, as one said: 'In matters of business, the Italian is a mountain-climber. He seeks footholds higher up.' They are firmly convinced, even so, that no corruption exists inside the Church courts.

In Paris, one wealthy Catholic discussed his experiences at the Rota in this connection with extreme frankness. He had obtained a difficult nullity decree without delay, and in consequence rumours had circulated that he had 'bought' his verdict. He insisted that this was a complete lie. Ignorant criticism of the Rota, he said, was damaging and insulting nonsense. 'Nowhere in the world,' he exclaimed, 'are there more men who are less easy to buy than these dedicated fathers of the Roman Catholic Church.'

He continued: 'Money does not enter into it. In fact, it can be a great mistake to try to make it do so, one of the very greatest mistakes. The judges of the Rota are smart men. They can scent a reason for a bribe, then make the offerer wish he had kept his mouth shut. You must not forget, even if you don't want to believe in the incorruptibility of the Vatican, that at least it is very rich. It does not need money offered illicitly to it; so much pours into its coffers from proper sources. No, believe me; to attempt to bribe these men is a most unintelligent thing to do!'

Unfortunately the purity of the Rota cannot excuse the corruption around it. Rome's apparent godlessness stems, in part, from conflict with the civil and criminal laws of Italy. These derive from the Church.

Just one example may be permitted. When a child is born of a Catholic Italian marriage, it is placed in its father's power. For the mother to seek an annulment of her marriage—even where she has a strong case—is to risk the near-certainty of losing her child if she is successful. Can anything more archaic be imagined? Yet it is the way Roman law bears down on the individual in response to the Church and, in consequence, corruption grows out of such oppression as naturally as mushrooms out of dung.

As the only possible means of escape, Rome's 'fixers' are always on hand with tempting offers to arrange any illegal service from false evidence to kidnapping, and those who resist their offers are often forced to suffer or flee. Diane Cilento, the actress, explained in London how she had ended her marriage to Andrea Volpi. He was the heir to a very wealthy Italian family fortune, they had been married in Italy in 1955, and she had had a daughter in 1957.

Miss Cilento said: 'I didn't want my child kept from me, so I refused to seek a nullity decree. I knew that, as she had been born in Italy, and as the father is given authority over the children there, it would have meant that I might easily lose her. I preferred to come back to London and divorce my husband civilly. Not that we had married in the Church.'

She added, with feeling: 'No, I had nothing to do with it. It's a big deal, that Rota; it costs more than I could afford.'

In this Miss Cilento may have been mistaken. Provided she had avoided corrupt lawyers, or 'fixers', her case need not have involved her in high costs. But the dangers of a young mother seeking satisfaction from this secretive, slow-moving court are not as they appear on the surface.

A woman whose married life has collapsed, whose child or children are being claimed by an estranged and alien husband and whose happiness is temporarily eclipsed, cannot be expected to act as sensibly as the celibate judges of the court demand. Yet if she fails to conform to their high standards she may prejudice her case. This is particularly true of a woman who has been persuaded into taking wrong or dishonest advice. The corruption net is waiting for such pathetic victims, and many are seen at the Rota. From them, the ungodliest of Romans enrich their pockets.

These weak women are guilty of serious sins. They have been parties to corruption and attempted forgery and faking of their cases. But the Church, too, must take some of the blame. Deliberate delay and secrecy in the courts is defended, on the grounds that they make it harder to obtain a nullity decree. But why should this be? What moral or ethical reasoning can back this assumption of power?

The Church claims to be the chosen instrument of God's authority. Has it also the right, thereby, to apply its own pressures? And where slowness and extreme secrecy can be shown to contribute, as they do, to a growing paganism on the doorstep of the Holy City, why cannot the Church show its wisdom by ending them, and freeing those caught in their toils? 'Ah, but the Church is a very wise old mother,' an English priest and canon lawyer told me. 'In whatever she does to preserve the letter of the law, men will always find a loophole, but she knows what is good for us!'

It is to be hoped that she also knows what is good for those who can no longer produce the spiritual austerity needed to seek the justice of her courts. For such as they, mercy is more urgently needed than wisdom.